KEVIN McCLOUD'S PRINCIPLES OF HOME

MAKING A PLACE TO LIVE

**Written in memory of my father
Donald McCloud, Engineer**

First published in hardback in 2010 by Collins
This abridged paperback edition first
published in 2011 by Collins

Collins

HarperCollins*Publishers*
77–85 Fulham Palace Road
London W6 8JB

www.harpercollins.co.uk

10 9 8 7 6 5 4 3 2 1

A catalogue record for this book is available from
the British Library.

ISBN: 978-0-00-742506-8

CONTENTS

This book is something of a manifesto for how we can live. It's a manifesto for a way of living that, in comparison with life of the last 60 years, could be slower, more enjoyable, gentler and altogether less taxing on the resources of this planet. It calls for a new appreciation of the human effort and energy that go into designing and making everything around us, from a spoon to a car, from a house to a city, from a dam to a cathedral. It calls for a re-evaluation of materials and fuel energy, and it calls for a culture in which we share much more of what we have in order that we don't squander it.

RO

I think we have lost touch with the made world. We have forgotten how difficult and time consuming it is to make something; how hard it is to make an elegant table out of a tree or a spoon out of metals dug out of the ground and refined. Our sensibilities to craftsmanship have been eroded by high-quality machine manufacturing; our tactile sense has been debased by artificial materials pretending to be something that they are not. Our attention, meanwhile, has been diverted by the virtual built worlds that exist inside screens. The landscapes of gaming and avatar worlds, for instance, are not complicated by the inconvenient messiness of the real world. In them, stuff, narratives, buildings and people are both perfect and disposable.

The real world is not perfect and it's not disposable. In the real world, things and people age and decompose. The real, tangible world is much harder to make, more difficult to maintain and unpleasant to recycle. Which may explain why so many people seek solace in virtual worlds, even if it's just by watching a soap opera on TV.

My Big Point is that I find the real world, which man has shaped, layered and renewed over thousands of years, more exciting and energizing – despite its grime – than any 3-D movie effect. Watching the Brooklyn Bridge explode in a computer-animated sequence may be awesome, but it is never as awe-inspiring as standing underneath the real thing and wondering how men managed to make it. Awesome is loud but awe is quiet.

I'm aware that my manifesto is motivated by a passionate love for places, buildings and things, not as objects that I want for myself to keep but as examples of human brilliance and creativity, the experience of which I want to share. I'm also frustrated, having worked as a designer and maker, by how little craftsmanship and the sweat of labour are appreciated nowadays. How we all assume that everything around us is made by machines and computers, whereas the truth is that your dinner plate was probably made by just three people in Portugal who spent four months of their lives producing a range for a high-street retailer; and your mobile phone was assembled by one person over a morning of their life.

So I'm writing out of a passionate love for the built environment and a quiet anger over how it is passed over in pursuit of temporary diversions and virtual pleasures when it can offer some of the greatest pleasures of all. The result goes something along the lines of: What do we want? A much better appreciation of the things around us so that we can cherish them, live a more sustainable life and enjoy a richer relationship with our world. When do we want it? Quite soon, please, and quickly. But not too quickly, because it's all meant to be about lingering to enjoy the moment, isn't it?

After the Slow Food movement, maybe it's time for the Slow Living movement. That sounds dull, doesn't it? In fact, 'slow' is the wrong word. It should be the Take Your Time movement (which is really what the Slow Food movement should be called). Take your time to appreciate what's around you, to explore your environment, to savour experiences and to develop relationships with the objects around you – be they a car, a vase or a town – as examples of human brilliance and human energy. In fact I do have a name for this softer, richer, more fulfilling experience. I call it New Materialism.

You'll have noticed that I slipped in that slippery word 'sustainable' earlier. It doesn't occur too often in this book because it's a term already over-used, so tried on by so many people, institutions and companies that it's stretched and gone all loose and floppy. Sustainability is now a big baggy sack into which people throw all kinds of old ideas, hot air and dodgy activities in order to be able to greenwash their products and feel good. Politicians speak of sustainable economic growth (this is not necessarily ecologically or socially beneficial), which is not the same thing as growing an economy sustainably.

This book doesn't deal with the fiscal or legal measures that will get us to a new 'sustainable' world, wherever that is. It suggests ways we can change ourselves that can make large differences. It won't beleaguer you with carbon calculators; it doesn't list fishing quotas or promote campaigns to save polar bears. You can join WWF or Friends of the Earth or Greenpeace, or subscribe to treehugger.com, if you want up-to-the-minute accounts of campaigns and government initiatives. My job here is to persuade you of something you might have overlooked: that your relationships with your possessions, your home and your street are the starting point for a new, more interesting way of experiencing the world and that the end result of that can be a significant reduction in your individual environmental impact.

It can mean more choice and more interesting choice as well. Let me give you an example, a real hot potato of an example. My company, Hab, builds homes in partnership with housing associations – the organizations who provide social housing – and we try to make our developments as ecological, enjoyable and socially progressive as possible. Hab stands for Happiness, Architecture, Beauty. It does not stand for Hummers, Audis and BMWs; which means, in pursuit of a way of life that is resource meagre and low carbon, we encourage residents to reduce their car use. We only provide one and a half parking spaces for each dwelling, which doesn't go down well with a lot of people. But in exchange for the one privation of one liberty – the right to park an unlimited number of vehicles wherever they want – residents get appealing alternatives including a car club and an intranet advising them of offers to share car journeys. The choice is limited in one way and enlarged in another. The emphasis is shifted from the personal and acquisitive to the communal and shared. That's what I mean by New Materialism: offering more choice, set in a different framework of choice.

That framework is composed of the ecological, environmental and social goals that many organizations and people are now working towards, from the social workers of Dharavi in India to the government of California.

It comprises ten goals, which reach far beyond governments' focus on carbon dioxide emissions, extend into every part of our lives and are based on an analysis of how we consume the world's resources. They're also very easy to understand: put simply, we have only one planet to support us, yet if everyone on the globe consumed as much and as fast as we do in the West, we'd need three planets to support us. Three planets of aluminium, forests, fish and fuel. But we have only one. There is no Planet B.

One Planet Living sets zero carbon as an objective and the great challenge of reducing our consumption of raw materials as another. It identifies waste, transport and food as problems. And it places mankind at the centre of its approach as not just the enemy of the environment but also part of that environment. We are not simply the problem; we ourselves are the victims. It is our species' happy survival that is at stake. So we also need to be the solution. Through technological advance, science, culture change and inventiveness, human energy might just solve the environmental and population problems we face.

ONE PLANET LIVING
OBJECTIVES

One Planet Living takes ten areas of our lives where we can creatively change what we do and where those decisions aren't necessarily restrictive but offer opportunities for an increase in the quality of our lives. If you're put off by the idea of change, I can reassure you that change means incorporating affordable, meaningful strategies into your life, strategies like deciding to buy food seasonally, growing your own, cutting down on your travel, retrofitting your home to be more comfortable and better insulated. The kinds of changes that can be made even more easily if you live in a sustainable and ecological development – like those that my company, Hab, is building. This book, among other things, explores those strategies. This book puts human beings at the centre.

1. Zero carbon
Making buildings more energy efficient and delivering all energy with renewable technologies.

2. Zero waste
Reducing waste, reusing where possible, and ultimately sending zero waste to landfill.

3. Sustainable transport
Encouraging low carbon modes of transport to reduce emissions, reducing the need to travel.

4. Sustainable materials
Using sustainable products that have a low embodied energy.

5. Local & sustainable food
Choosing low impact, local, seasonal and organic diets and reducing food waste.

6. Sustainable water
Using water more efficiently in buildings and in the products we buy; tackling local flooding and water course pollution.

7. Natural habitats & wildlife
Protecting and expanding old habitats and creating new space for wildlife.

8. Cultural heritage
Reviving local identity and wisdom; support for, and participation in, the arts.

9. Equity, fair trade & local economy
Inclusive, empowering workplaces with equitable pay; support for local communities and fair trade.

10. Health & happiness
Encouraging active, sociable, meaningful lives to promote good health and well being.

Finished houses at The Triangle, the first Hab Housing project in Swindon

PRINCIPLE
01

Demand that your home consumes the minimum of energy yet keeps you warm and comfortable. Demand a healthy environment with fresh, clean air. Demand that your building does not just save energy but produces it. Demand that your home has a minimal environmental footprint and uses our precious resources wisely and sparingly.

Sunlight House, Pressbaum, near Vienna – the first carbon-neutral one-family house in Austria

I hope my book will help you value the material world in a different, fuller way. I hope that as you read it, you'll begin to wonder where it was made, who by and how much paper, ink, solvent, glue, machine maintenance, shipping, packaging, handling and energy it took to make it; how much time, effort and care were spent by the dozens of people who were involved with it. And I hope that, as well as awakening your curiosity, it will give you the tools for minimizing our detrimental impact on the environment and on other human beings: the tools of wasting less (or wasting nothing), saving fuel energy, exploiting what we have to hand, respecting craftsmanship, reusing the resources and made things that we already have, and sharing them more.

Threading throughout the entire book are the 43 Principles of Home, memorable ideas which I've collected or formulated over the past 30 years, drawing inspiration from the best of Le Corbusier, Vitruvius, William Morris and Homer Simpson.

TEST ONE: WHICH IS THE MOST ENVIRONMENTALLY FRIENDLY HOUSE?

A. A 500-year-old farmhouse, built from local materials – any stones that were just turned up out of the field – and oak trees from the farm in which it sits, with stone floors laid on the earth and thick walls with a high thermal mass. Albeit the place is listed and hasn't got double glazing.

B. A house built by Ben Law in the forest in Sussex, entirely from the forest in Sussex. Ben cut 10,000 shingles from his own coppiced chestnut trees. The frame is coppiced chestnut and the oak cladding, straw-bale insulation and ash window frames are all from his woods and cut and assembled by him. This place does have double glazing, and it's off grid, has its own water supply and is heated by Ben's own wood thinnings from his sustainable forestry business, making charcoal and hurdles.

C. A three-bedroom family home in Scotland. It has super-insulated walls, it's airtight, it has a state-of-the-art Panelvent timber panel construction sitting on a concrete plinth for high thermal mass, it's triple-glazed and it comes with a heat recovery system.

So which is greener than green? Well, it has to be Ben's, of course. Maybe followed by the Scottish timber box. With the farmhouse a poor third, maybe. Which, it turns out, has no oil-fired range, has 10 inches of loft insulation and is heated with a biomass boiler.

Answer: Again, it's down to use. You can construct a super-insulated, resource-meagre dwelling, turn the heating up and then open all the windows. Or live in a freezing mansion with no heating and one bath a week. There is no such thing as an eco-home, just as there's no such thing as an eco-car. It's our use of these things that determines not how environmentally friendly they are but how environmentally friendly we are.

TEST TWO: WHICH IS THE MOST ECO-FRIENDLY CAR IN THE LIST BELOW?

A. A Toyota Prius
B. A 1937 Alfa Romeo tourer
C. A Ferrari
D. A 37-year-old Bond 875 (my first car)
E. The Innocent Smoothie van
F. An Aston Martin DB9
G. A Range Rover

You might plump for the Prius as the angel of the pack and the Range Rover as the devil. Let me ask you another question: if you had the money, would you commission a small firm of English cabinet-makers to make you a bespoke, crafted piece of furniture? Or buy a cheap copy from the Far East? Well, the more ethical solution has to be the former: it's a local transaction, it involves much less shipping, it creates relationships between the makers and the owner. The automotive equivalent is buying an Aston Martin over a Toyota Prius.

Surely this is rubbish. The Prius emits 145 grams of carbon per kilometre while the Aston emits nearly 500. But even these figures are meaningless. Who is the biggest environmental sinner? The man who drives his Prius 20 miles to and from work each day? Or the man who travels 50 miles on the train? Or the man who owns an Aston Martin and walks across his yard to his office and drives his car at weekends only? It's probably the Prius driver.

Answer: This is just an exercise to point out that whatever you think of executive SUVs, hybrid cars and GT sports cars, calculating the environmental impact of these vehicles is very complex and ultimately dependent much more on how we use our vehicles than how big their engines are or where they were built.

PART
ONE
ENE[

RGY

Chapter One

SETTING FIRE TO THINGS

There are those days when the sun just hammers down through a blue sky and you think to yourself what a fine day for a barbecue. At least you do if you're an unreformed male who jumps at every opportunity to reach back into the cave and set fire to something.

B-B-Q-ing is a man thing: an atavistic chest-banging, wandering-around-the-woods-sniffing-each-other's-bottoms thing that connects male human beings to their pasts and the pasts of all their friends and their friends' bottoms. Barbecues have done more for the social integrity of our modern world than all the Round Tables and Working Men's Clubs put together. Alcohol may play a part. But the tradition of overcooking food on an uncontrollable open fire is a venerable social glue.

WOOD BURNERS

I like to think that fire has elevated me from the level of 'beast' to my special status as a human being. I have a good relationship with fire. At home I have three woodburners to heat my house, which consume timber that I grow on my farm. Three years ago I installed a 120-kilowatt Austrian woodchip burner to heat the whole farm, including outbuildings and offices. It runs on chipped waste timber from things like broken pallets and burns the stuff with the same gusto and noise as a Eurofighter Typhoon on

afterburn. I've got my own miniature inferno to play with.

One of my woodburners is a Franklin, designed to sit in a large inglenook, and I'm fond of it. It has doors that can be left open to enjoy the flames or shut to keep a fire in overnight. Separate sliding plates govern how much air can be let in for combustion and how large the exhaust port is. Together with the doors, these plates minutely control what happens inside the stove and have been the stock-in-trade features of any and every cast-iron

woodburner ever made. Except Benjamin Franklin, the 18th-century inventor, figured it out first. His lifetime's letters are peppered with correspondence with gentlemen from all over the globe seeking to improve the efficiency of their homes' heating: how they might stop their rooms from being choked with smoke when the wind changes direction; how they might get better value out of their fuel and live more comfortably and safely. And for Franklin, it seems that dealing with this steady barrage of requests was, if anything, a pleasure.

Franklin might be amused to see how his invention, a metal chamber in which wood could be burnt more efficiently and controllably, would come to be seen as the first internal combustion machine. Its descendants power our cars and planes. But I think he would equally be aghast at how we take fuel for granted now. In Franklin's time you either had to chop down a tree (which would warm you once), stack the wood (warming you twice) and then bring it indoors to burn. Or you had to pay someone to do it for you, leaving a cold, empty feeling in the wallet. Either way you had direct contact with the fuel, its source and the human energy required to get it as far as the hearth. And not surprisingly you were interested in as many means of making that process more efficient, and in getting as much heat out of the fuel as possible. Nowadays fuel comes through rubber hoses from underground tanks or out of an electrical socket. Franklin would have loved the ease with which fuels can get to our homes. But he would have scratched his head at the fuel inefficiency of a 4-litre Porsche Cayenne. He might even have wondered why he'd bothered.

But there is still something to be said for the inefficiency and beauty of an open fire – which is why Benjamin designed my stove with big folding front doors that can be opened. If you enjoy looking at the flames of an open hearth licking up the chimney, then you should make a visit to a blacksmith's forge. You'll see and hear material combust as though in the Devil's own crucible.

Now fuel's visible and symbolic roles in the hearth and incense burner have been replaced by more covert and mundane roles. And more diverse too. Whereas we once kept a couple of coal or wood fires going at home in the kitchen range and drawing-room fireplace, today we might have a condensing gas boiler for heat, cook on electricity from a nuclear or diesel or coal-fired power station and drive a car that runs on gasoline – or maybe bioethanol if we're progressive and American. Generally, our fuel use is far more sophisticated and freely available. About the only thing we burn as primitively as we did then is tobacco. Oh, and charcoal in the barbecue. We use more fuels to live faster, more luxurious lives, but don't know anything about those fuels or where they come

from. Nor, it seems, do we care. And consequently we're finding it rather hard to accept what all that burning might be doing to our atmosphere.

You might be forgiven for thinking that, in attempting to persuade you that burning things is not only good but also part of the earth's natural systems, I'm encouraging us all to go out and burn more. I'm not. I'm just making the point that, despite our relationship to all kinds of fuel being an honourable one, we have forgotten what fuel is and where it comes from. Just as children nowadays think that fish are rectangular and orange and come in boxes, so adults believe that petrol is an alien, synthesized chemical that comes out of a hose from a tank in the ground to be briefly glimpsed and smelt on its way into the bowels of your 4x4. We don't understand petrol; we don't even see it being burnt. It's a fossil fuel, but when we use those words what we really should be saying is that petrol comes from the trees and plants that rotted hundreds of millions of years ago to make our coal and gas and oil reserves. They are all the products of photosynthesis. Plant growth is what keeps us warm, fed, moving and clothed, and we shouldn't forget it.

CHARCOAL

Charcoal has a certain magic to it, an alchemical quality. Scientists call charcoal the solid carbon residue following pyrolysis (carbonization or destructive distillation) of carbonaceous raw materials. Which is accurate but incomprehensible. I call charcoal the miracle transformation from useless wood into an extraordinarily useful fuel.

The reason I say 'useless fuel' is that the majority of timbers, like petrol, go up in flames and that's it. The bulk of the heat produced is carried by the convection currents that the heat produces. Whereas what we like is for heat to be radiated out in straight lines to warm us and our dogs and to heat our pans. So oak, for example, burns well but disintegrates the moment it's combusted, leaving just a pile of white ash. Useless. Willow burns badly and spits to boot, although this does mean it might set fire to your house, resulting in a really good warming glow. Worse than useless. Ash is called the king of firewoods because having been burnt it doesn't disintegrate, leaving instead a red-hot glowing ember that produces masses of radiant heat. That's more like it.

Two clever things about charcoal:
1. It can be made from almost any wood, including oak, willow, hickory, nutshells and even fruit pips – or for that matter vegetable waste and paper mill residues.

2. The tars and resins present in the fuel have been burnt off, so what you get is 100 per cent ready-to-light carbon embers that radiate enormous amounts of energy.

Historically, charcoal has been very useful. It was burnt 6,000 years ago for smelting copper, and then iron after the invention of the blast furnace around AD 1400. The big domestic change happened in the 1920s, when Henry Ford invented the charcoal briquette, using scrap wood and sawdust as his ingredients. The Ford car (invented, incidentally, to burn bioethanol from maize, not petrol) was merely a sideline for Ford, something that would get people to drive out of town and experiment with his briquettes. Proof of this, should you want it, is that a good number of his car dealerships devoted half their sales floor space to charcoal equipment and cooking supplies. It demonstrates a rare example of synergy genius in manufacturing: creating a product (the car) and the reason to use that product (recreational outdoor cookery) by the same stroke.

It also explains the long-standing tradition of charcoal being sold on garage forecourts and why charcoal is made in giant industrial plants now. The traditional batch method involves loading a circular container (they use concrete kilns these days) with timber and then setting fire to it in a very controlled way, regulating the air that gets to it, for up to a week. The load then has to cool for up to two weeks. Hopeless if you've got to produce a million tonnes a year, which is why the Continuous Process was invented for the manufacture of Henry Ford's briquettes. This starts with sizing, where timber is broken up into standard dimensions (a 3mm particle size is one standard) in a hammer mill and often mixed with sawdust or bark.

The wood is then dried to a consistent moisture content of about 25 per cent (roughly half its wet, freshly cut content) and then dropped into a multiple hearth retort, a giant furnace that resembles a steel silo divided internally into floors. Which is why I wanted to learn how to make charcoal properly.

02

Sustainability is not a bolt-on, nor a government department, but a culture: a way of doing things.

BEN'S WAY

In my romantic, back-to-nature-bottom-sniffing way, I have always dreamed of a hard-core existence, where I would depend on nature for survival, make my bed under a bush, collect berries and dig for roots. I usually have this dream while lying in my bed under a silk and wool duvet on crisp linen sheets. In the middle of a chestnut forest somewhere in Sussex lives someone who has done a great deal more than just dream. In 2002 Ben Law built a house in the woods, a beautiful timber-clad, round-pole-framed, straw-bale-insulated, two-storey house, and I made an hour-long television programme about its design and construction.

If you're reading this on the train on the way to work, or in the comfort of a centrally heated house, you may find the idea of living in the woods and depending on the environment around you for food, water, power, warmth and solace terrifying. You might wonder what you'd do without a freezer or an iPod or a hot bath. But Ben has all of these things. He runs a small fridge/freezer from power stored in a bank of old submarine batteries and generated by two small wind turbines and an array of second-hand photovoltaic cells

that had previously graced the roof of the Big Brother house (first series). He can light and power the house (all on 12 volts) enough to provide all the music and entertainment he and his young family need. His wood-powered Rayburn stove heats the kitchen and the hot water (collected from the roof) to provide steaming hot baths. Oh – and the old bathwater is run off to water the vegetable garden while the wood for fuel is, of course, free.

Ben doesn't have to get the train to work, either. He can walk out of his door and go and chop some wood, make some furniture to sell, weave a hurdle or two or make charcoal. He now runs a successful business selling the products made from his forest, all of which are renewable products, not just because they're made from trees – which can be replanted – but because they're made from coppiced trees.

Ben is an underwoodsman, an altogether shyer profession of tree-cutter who makes his living mainly from the 'underwood', not from the majestic canopy of the forest but from those smaller trees than can be cropped again and again. This is coppicing, a process not unlike pollarding, where a tree is cut back to its trunk.

LEFT: The living room in Ben's house

Constable's paintings are full of willows growing by the River Stour in Suffolk that have been pollarded repeatedly, giving them enormous sturdy trunks topped with a younger growth of more supple branches. Every few years, trees like this can be cut ruthlessly back to a stump 2 metres or so high, providing fuel, and long, bendy willow whips that can be formed into hurdles or basketry. The stump survives, grows more shoots and regrows quickly, thanks to the extensive root system that the tree has. It becomes an endless supply of material, the tree is prevented from ageing and the river is kept clear of unwanted overhanging foliage and boughs.

Coppicing is even more ruthless. Certain species owf tree, notably willow, hazel, hickory, ash and sweet chestnut, will tolerate being cut right down to the ground once the tree has lost its leaves and shut down for the winter. Next spring a new crop of fast-growing and straight poles will spring from the stump, which in five or ten or twenty years can once more be harvested. Again, because of the developed root system, growth can be prodigious.

Coppicing is a form of natural magic. It defies belief, given that when you chop down a fir tree or spruce that's it: the tree doesn't regrow and neither does anything else there for a while. But in a coppiced woodland, as the stump quickly regrows, so do vetches and violets in the newfound warmth and light of the clearing. As the poles grow into a bush, nightingales, turtle doves and dormice are attracted. Later, flycatchers will dart around the tall airy poles of a well-managed copse. Some species are even totally dependent on coppicing for their survival, like the pearl-bordered fritillary, a now-threatened species of butterfly.

From coppiced poles you can make an enormous variety of useful things, using all kinds of timbers. Hazel rods have historically been used for everything from dowsing sticks to thatching spars to the split rods that form the wattle in wattle and daub. An especially fast-growing form of willow, osier, or *Salix viminalis*, is still cropped for basket-weaving. Ben built his round-pole house from coppiced chestnut and very probably most of the timber he harvested has now regrown, locking more carbon into its structure. His is a carbon-invisible house. Apart from the elegant furniture and hurdles that he makes from the same chestnut, the brash (small branchlets and twigs) are sold to the Environment Agency for riverbank reinforcement.

And after the handles and poles and brash and pegs and spars and furniture and hurdles are produced the remaining bits and bobs are chopped and sized for, yes, charcoal making.

Ben won planning consent for his house in the middle of the woods precisely because he makes charcoal. Unlike conventional forestry, which you can do between the hours of nine and five, charcoal burning requires that you stay near the furnace to control it and prevent any wildfire, which could be catastrophic in a wood. Ben argued that although there was no planning precedent, he should be allowed to build effectively in open countryside, just as a farmer can if he can demonstrate the need for an agriculturally tied dwelling. After seven years, Ben won, the only catch being that if he ever sells the wood and retires, he has to demolish the house. Needless to say he is tirelessly fighting that condition.

PRINCIPLE
03

A sustainable way of life means not a diminution of choices but a change of choices and an increase. It can be measured not in terms of standard of living but in quality of life.

04

ENERGY CRISIS

People do not enjoy constancy and relish the opportunity to react to changes in the environment, to breezes and changes in temperature. We are biologically programmed to enjoy this reaction and become bored if our home and working environments are kept static.

Between 1930 and 1990, the amount of energy available to us on the planet increased eightfold. And in the last 100 years the price of energy relative to almost everything else has dropped tenfold. That makes it sound as though we're living inside a gasoline explosion, which to some extent we are. The laptop that I'm writing this on, the plastic water bottle beside you, your mobile phone and fleece, the paint on your walls and the acrylic tiles on your floor are all made out of crude oil, out of the cheap components of oil that get left over after the petroleum and diesel and other fuels have been distilled off. These are also things that would otherwise be prohibitively expensive, were it not for the even cheaper petroleum and diesel that generate the energy to make them. This cheapness makes the availability of all these goods seem miraculous. Which, in terms of the giant network of industries, processes and companies needed to process the goo and transform it into clever products, it is. Ours is a petroleum world. Crude oil gives us a standard of

living that we could not have dreamed of 100 years ago. The only trouble is that the oil is slowly running out.

True, no one quite knows for sure when oil production will peak; everyone will know once it's happened. It might be happening now. Meanwhile, untapped reserves under the polar caps may delay the onset of fossil fuel decline.

According to some sources, oil discoveries peaked in 1965 and peak oil production per capita peaked in 1979. Industry pessimists think that we're reaching the global consumption peak more or less right now.

And if we're running out of conventional oil reserves, there are some pretty unconventional resources yet to be exploited, including a lot more coal.

The essential problem in all of this is that when we dig or suck fossil fuels out of the ground and set fire to them in metal boxes of one kind or another, we are consuming stored energy that was laid down millions of years ago as plants decayed. It was originally energy from the sun that

LEFT: Part of the Romford Road key worker social housing development in East London, designed by architect Stock Woolstencroft

was trapped and converted through photosynthesis. That process is the same process that stored the energy in the sawdust that's used to make charcoal briquettes. It's the same process that Ben Law's coppiced chestnut trees use to lock energy into their fast-growing stems, so that Ben can build his house out of poles and make his charcoal free of any guilt of the wastefulness of all that burning of a summer's evening because his trees grow faster and absorb more carbon dioxide than he can ever produce there.

Meanwhile, the carbon dioxide that is released through burning fossil fuels, the carbon dioxode that is emitted into the atmosphere and then contributes to the greenhouse effect and climate change, the carbon dioxide that's a by-product of us gobbling up that huge time-banked reserve of solar energy that is buried under the ground, just hangs around.

If we all burned wood and charcoal, and replanted and regrew timber for our needs, then we wouldn't be in the mess we're in. But with nearly seven billion people on the planet and that figure growing, chances are we couldn't meet our needs or anything

like them. Fossil fuels have been the obvious solution for hundreds of years now. They're cheap but they are the reserves into which we should perhaps never have dipped. There is no way we can plant enough trees to absorb the carbon outputs of fuels which, although starting life as biomass or timber, have remained locked away in vast quantities, only to be released in one powerful and very short burst of 200 years against the millions of years it took to lay down the deposits and the hundreds of millions of years during which they've remained untouched.

Conventional oil production might have peaked, but there's a few more decades' worth left. Coal and gas offer a long-term seductive offer (it's possible, thanks to German technology invented during the Second World War, to extract pretty much everything found in oil from coal as well). If we carry on burning fuels at today's rate, we might have enough fossil fuel for 600 years. So there is in fact plenty there. The trouble is we hit big, big environmental trouble in 50 or 60 years.

According to the American Energy Information Administration (EIA), worldwide energy consumption

is growing at 2 per cent a year. Hey! 2 per cent! That's nothing! Except that when you compound that percentage it means that our energy needs double every 35 years.

With fuel usage growing at 2 per cent a year it turns out we'll have no more fossil fuel of any kind on the planet within 150 years. More worryingly, the point at which we go off the rails, where temperature increase is no longer controllable (where we go above that 2°C rise and where we've pumped our maximum allowance of 400 billion tonnes of carbon into the atmosphere), is going to come much sooner.

Despite Kyoto, Rio and Copenhagen summits, despite the continuing warnings that we must contain atmospheric carbon to within 350 parts per million to avoid tripping over the 2°C rise, despite some governments' commitment to reducing carbon dioxide output by 80 per cent before 2050, everything's going in the other direction. According to the Pew Center on Global Climate Change, carbon dioxide (CO_2) emissions have, since 2000, increased 33 per cent faster than in the 1990s.

The 2005 US Department of Energy report known as the

Hirsch report predicted that oil peaking is likely to lead to abrupt consequences for oil-dependent economies. But the report also optimistically predicts that we can make the transition to a low-fossil-fuel economy with enough time and preparation. By which it means 20 years and a colossal effort on the part of governments. It might be possible. Researchers at the Swedish University of Agricultural Sciences estimate that globally we use only about 20 per cent of the biomass (energy crops such as timber, elephant grass or hemp) that can be sustainably produced and that it might be possible to provide a third of the planet's energy needs from biomass through both direct burning of that material and the creation from them of what are called 'densified biofuels'.

And the great plus of growing sustainable crops for fuel is that they lock the sun's energy into woody material, together with absorbed atmospheric carbon dioxide. What they release in burning they absorb in growing, which makes a satisfying ecological balance sheet. In contrast, extracting reserves from under the ground and releasing the sun's energy and atmospheric

CO_2 from 300 million years ago – well, that's trading on a big overdraft.

Some individuals within the energy industry are placing great store by carbon sequestration: they want to see oil and coal reserves fully exploited and the problem dealt with at the point of combustion – although the technology to lock enormous quantities of CO_2 either underground or in outer space is currently about as successful as the anti-gravity hover car. Nobody's got it to work on a commercial scale. Elsewhere, campaigners like Al Gore are parading their doom-mongering, which is now becoming so pervasive across our newspapers and screens that pretty soon we're all going to get Armageddon fatigue. Others believe we still have time, just, to initiate a giant plan of renewable energy. James Lovelock, inventor of the Gaia theory, has suggested that it is already too late and that we should be embracing nuclear power with all haste. The ludicrous Danish economist Bjørn Lomborg thinks we should dump Kyoto and spend the three trillion dollars it would cost to implement it on tidal barrages and fresh drinking water for

the whole world.

There are reasons why some of these plans may not work. Almost every environmental problem in the world is about resources: about man's pressure on the ability of the planet to provide and regenerate enough clean air, water, fuel, food and minerals to sustain us and every other creature on earth. The bigger the global population, the greater the pressure. We're running out of almost everything we need.

So which future are you betting your pension on? Which future has your pension company bet your pension on? Do you think technology can deliver miracle solutions? Well, it might if we had 100 years to play with, but we don't. We've got a couple of decades, in fact. Do you think that through efficiency, with leaner-burn jet engines and super-insulated homes, we can reduce our carbon footprints and carry on travelling to the Maldives for our holidays? Possibly, but if every human were to enjoy that kind of holiday the Maldives would be under water in 20 years. So should we all live like Ben, build a composting loo and learn how to cook Nettle Bake?

05

Organize your home life around who you are and what you do. If you have a family, enshrine what is good about that family in the layout of your building. If you're single, enjoy it while you can.

SO WHAT NOW?

In the introduction I emphasized how the very definition of sustainability wasn't about saving the planet but about saving humanity. And to do that human beings are going to have to once again visit their own extraordinary reserves of inventiveness and energy. We have two saving graces that might just protect us. One is our resourcefulness; the other is our imagination. It is those two facilities that have, for millennia, got us out of the merde or got things really motoring. They got both Ben Law and Henry Ford into the charcoal business. Resourcefulness and imagination led to new technologies, new efficiencies and even new ways of living.

For the past ten years I've made films and series about the adventures people go on when they try to improve their environment by building something or regenerating their neighbourhood. I've seen resourcefulness and imagination at work and they are blindingly powerful energies. They're the energies that have always led us to try to create better futures within the natural environment that

the planet offers. That's what architecture is: an attempt at a better, more comfortable and sometimes more equitable world.

Last time I went to the supermarket I had a choice between buying the own-brand charcoal for my barbie and another brand in a brightly coloured green bag. When I looked at the small print on the own-brand bag it turned out that the contents came from South Africa. South African charcoal. Shipped all the way to the UK just to be set fire to.

Meanwhile the British countryside is overburdened with copses and traditional woodlands which for centuries were coppiced and maintained, introducing light to the woodland floor and increasing biodiversity. Now we're ignoring them, allowing these places to deteriorate into low-grade scrubland. The British countryside is the home of coppicing; we virtually invented it. And we can't be bothered with it any more.

I've already said that there are two magical properties of charcoal: that it can be made from almost

any wood and that it comes in a lightweight, ready-to-glow form. But there is a third alchemical quality to it that can be nowadays exploited in modern 'pyrolysis' high-temperature furnaces and woodburners. When you heat woody material beyond 270°C the tars and gases in the timber burn off, leaving you with charcoal. That's how the stuff is made. But what if you could use the heat from that burn-off for something useful like heating homes or generating electricity? And since charcoal is effectively just the carbon content of wood, the condensed remains of all the CO_2 that a tree or plant absorbed in its life, isn't there a way of locking that CO_2 into the earth by not setting fire to it on the hearth? Is there a way that charcoal can be used as an alchemical CO_2 sink?

Together with his colleagues, Dr Gabriel Gallagher of Sustainable Energy Limited has researched the potential of bio-char to lock up or 'sequester' large amounts of atmospheric CO_2 and calculated that 1 hectare of biomass – which could be hemp or coppice woodland,

for example – might generate every year 1,350 kilowatts of electricity, 5,400 kilowatts of heat and 4 tonnes of CO_2 sequestered in the remaining charcoal.

When felled and used for construction, materials like timber and hemp insulation lock carbon into the building, removing it from the atmosphere. The bad news is that a dead tree in the forest generally decomposes in the air, producing a variety of gases that include much of the carbon in its structure. We don't and can't use all the timber around us for construction; not all of it is suitable. We're not chopping enough trees down to use, and we're perhaps not making enough charcoal either.

Charcoal is our last, dirty, dusty connection with the life of our ancestors, and the most tenuous link to helping us remember the value of our energy.

So it's a good thing to burn the sausages of a Sunday lunchtime. It's a good thing to spuriously set fire to something now and again. It reminds us how magical flames are, inside the metal box or outside.

Chapter Two

ENERGY IN YOUR WALLS

There are three ways of looking at a building's ability to keep you warm, lit, cosy, entertained and fed (all of which boil down to its ability to manage all the gas, oil, wood and electricity that you feed into it). You can see the building as a shell, a protective covering that you pump full of energy and hope will keep hold of it long enough for you to cook an evening meal, watch some TV and then have a hot bath.

That, frankly, is how most of the world's population — in even the most civilized of countries — think of the home they live in. If you're an enlightened individual with an eye on your wallet and an interest in lowering your fuel bills, you'll see the structure of your dwelling as a leaky sieve that needs to be stopped up with insulation and draught excluders to keep the interior warm in winter. If you're committed about the third way, both saving money and the environmental impact of your home, it gets a little more complicated.

But not a lot. The simple evaluations of how environmentally friendly a building is have been codified and complicated by engineers and governments, who need to measure and quantify minimum standards, but essentially, a good, ecological building is made from as much recycled material as possible that has had as little environmental impact as possible and which is as healthy as possible to live in. It might also be highly recyclable itself. It would probably be fairly modest in scale and size too, to further minimize impact.

If you were to further analyse the materials used for the building, you might begin to separate out the chemical/waste/transport effects from the energy input used to make the stuff. What you would find is that, generally, the healthier and more planet-lite a material is, the less energy and fossil fuel is required to manufacture it. Sheep's wool insulation and laminated timber beams are two good examples. It's a rule of thumb.

But the big debates in sustainable construction do not rage around whether to use sheep's wool, rockwool or bellybutton fluff. They don't even batter the issues of recycling and the embodied energy. They devote pretty well all their focus to the problem of how much energy a building uses during its lifetime.

This is important, of course. The argument runs that it is better and easier to devise the mass production of affordable synthetic loft insulation made from petrochemicals than it is to persuade everybody to become instantly ecological. The argument suggests that people will always be persuaded to save money and fuel sooner than they will adapt or accept culture change. And when you look at the figures that relate a building's embodied construction energy to its in-use consumption of energy, the argument becomes irresistible.

I once made a programme about a young couple building an earth-sheltered home in northern England in the Cumbrian fells, where the rain falls and the wind blows a lot. This was a three-bedroomed modest house set into a hill, with a sloping front wall of glass that contained a thermal 'heat space' or full-height lobby behind it, for trapping solar energy. They installed a wind turbine and photovoltaic panels in order to be minimally dependent on the electricity grid. And because they built their home into a big wet English hill, they built it from waterproof concrete.

Concrete is one of the bad boys of construction. Every tonne of cement, the glue that makes concrete set, produces a tonne of carbon dioxide (CO_2) in manufacture: half of that is due to the fuel needed to heat cement's constituents, chalk or limestone and clay, to form clinker; half is due to the chemical reaction between the chalk and the clay where CO_2 is the by-product. There are ecological versions of concrete, but pretty well all of them are shades of grey rather than green.

Phil and Helen's home, though not large, still needed around 500 tonnes of concrete. Working on the back of a fag packet, we calculated together that the cement content was around 50 tonnes, meaning 50 tonnes of carbon. Given the paint, glazing, timber and other materials in the building, we generously doubled that and then figured out that, with the building's reduced impact on the grid and its super-insulated, super-protected, earth-sheltered structure, it would take between 12 and 16 years for the energy and CO_2 input to be balanced out – 14 years, say, for that concrete hulk to become carbon neutral because the building was energy efficient in use.

The built world is responsible for generating up to 60 per cent of our CO_2 emissions, most of which comes from the occupation, heating and cooling of buildings. But cement production represents a significant fraction of that 60 per cent: it's responsible for between 7 and 10 per cent of total emissions worldwide and it's rising. Cement rivals air travel for environmental impact.

Cement is an easy example for us to look at because of its tangible impact and because its use in concrete is so widespread. And like it or not, concrete is here to stay. You might as well like it, because apart from being an extraordinarily plastic material from which architects can form fabulous shapes and breathtaking buildings, without it we'd have no dams or cooling towers, no Eddystone Lighthouse, nuclear power stations, sea defences, Eurotunnel or Millau Viaduct. And your house would have no foundations.

There is another compelling argument for using concrete, other than for structural strength, and that's thermal mass. Insulation isn't the only way of keeping heat in a building: big heavy walls can help. Big heavy walls have mass and when they're made from earth, stone or concrete, the slow heaviness of them makes them recalcitrant and lumbering. They absorb heat slowly, store it and then release it slowly in the same way a night storage heater does in its heavy thermal bricks. These materials do it so well that they help regulate the temperature in a building around the clock and even around the year. I know because my own home has stone walls 3 feet thick in places. With the windows and doors draughtproofed, I can be confident that once I've got the place heated in winter it will stay reasonably comfortable without quick fluctuations in air temperature.

I can also look forward to a cool building on the hottest day of the year because walls with thermal mass resist overheating in the sun, transmitting that solar energy just as slowly as the heat from my woodburner. This is an advantage that a well-insulated timber frame just doesn't have; indeed the major criticism of timber construction in temperate and warmer latitudes is that, with climate change leading to potentially warmer summers, the lack of thermal mass in timber buildings will lead them to overheat.

My home doesn't have any insulation. It has no cavity; it has old plaster on the inside and a rubble stone finish to the exterior. It is also listed, which means I cannot interfere with any of this. In an ideal world I would insulate the place with a thick overcoat, not inside but outside. I would envelop the thermal mass of all that stone with a duvet of some kind, to slow its leakage of heat right down and exploit the fact that the bulk of the energy that I want to put into the wall and take out of it could then be controlled from inside the building using solar gain through imaginary big triple-glazed windows and my woodburner.

I can't do that because I'm a sucker for old buildings, so I have a large collection of pullovers. Here are some important ways of managing the structure of your home – whether new or old – as a means of minimizing the building's embodied and day-to-day energy patterns.

LOOK INTO THE EYES OF YOUR HOME

Architecture and the design process are the most streamlined and time-honoured processes for the delivery of environments of the highest quality and provide proven 'fertile ground' for sustainability.

My ancient home is single glazed and it doesn't have big windows; big windows facing south (in the northern hemisphere) are an ideal component in heavy thermal mass buildings. Of course glass is a terrible thermal insulator because it's a relatively efficient conductor of heat, making windows an exemplary way of warming the planet. Our buildings lose an embarrassing quantity of heat through glass (not least because a window is a lot thinner than a brick) and so, not surprisingly, the glazing industry has responded by lobbying for a change in the way glazing's thermal performance is assessed. It has argued (rightly) that building regulations should take into account the ability of glass to transmit infrared

energy from the sun into a building, where it can be stored as heat in the heavy thermal mass of, say, a concrete plinth or stone floor. This is a free and easy way of getting energy into the structure of a building and then exploiting the thermal mass to store it there for as long as possible.

As far as my old place is concerned, small windows at least mean a smaller heat loss – something I've mitigated by fitting heavy curtains, having shutters made (traditional timber shutters have a very significant effect on heat loss through glazing) and ordering insulating blinds from the brilliant Heatsaver blind company, whose fabric blinds have the same effect as installing 85mm of fibreglass insulation.

PLANT A TREE

Architects spend their time plotting solar paths and zeniths for the purpose of figuring out just how big their overhangs should be in summer. The argument runs that a window should allow light and solar heat into a building in winter when the sun is low but be sufficiently shaded in warmer months when the sun is higher.

So said architects design exciting-looking brise-soleil panels above doors and windows as part of the architectural language of the building. You could instead plant a tree: a small deciduous one, such as a full-standard apple tree, which would lose its leaves in the winter but provide dappled cool shade in the summer.

REMEMBER TO BREATHE

To be fair, this is not a method for trapping winter solar and man-made heat in the building's fabric but a summer solution for getting rid of too much heat in your home's structure. If your building overheats, see whether you can adapt it into a breeze chimney. This is a technique often found in ancient Persian construction, where buildings were fitted with wind towers. Air movement around the top of the towers would suck air out of the building, allowing it to be drawn in from vents that were often connected to underground canals or buried air ducts.

Alternatively, when heated by the intense effect of the sun on the masonry, the air inside the towers would rise, sucking in air from below and again drawing in cooler air. This made it possible to cool the interior of these masonry buildings to almost frigid temperatures.

My company's first housing project used this technology to keep the homes cool in summer. Each home is fitted with a rooftop vent instead of a chimney, as well as small vents around the building that can be securely left open during the day. As the home warms during the day, the hot air rises and leaves the building, and cooler air is drawn in from ground level.

You can improvise your own system by adapting an existing first-floor chimney or just adapting existing windows with security fittings so that they can be left propped open but secure. And maybe dig a little pond next to the house. By drawing the incoming air over water, the air is humidified and further cooled.

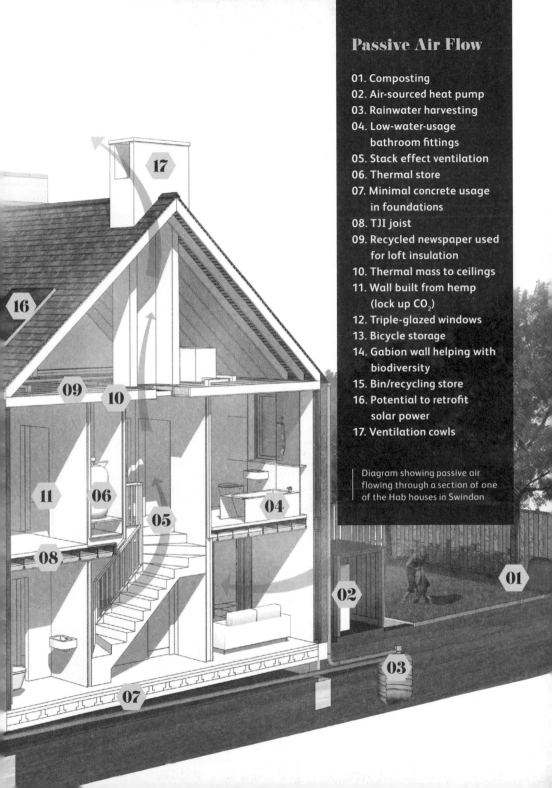

Passive Air Flow

01. Composting
02. Air-sourced heat pump
03. Rainwater harvesting
04. Low-water-usage bathroom fittings
05. Stack effect ventilation
06. Thermal store
07. Minimal concrete usage in foundations
08. TJI joist
09. Recycled newspaper used for loft insulation
10. Thermal mass to ceilings
11. Wall built from hemp (lock up CO_2)
12. Triple-glazed windows
13. Bicycle storage
14. Gabion wall helping with biodiversity
15. Bin/recycling store
16. Potential to retrofit solar power
17. Ventilation cowls

Diagram showing passive air flowing through a section of one of the Hab houses in Swindon

ECO-CONCRETES ... ISH

When I was installing my woodchip boiler, I needed a reinforced base to support the 'thermal buffer' water tanks, the boiler unit and the 90-cubic-metre chipstore. My local (and ethical) builders' merchants had the answer: eco-concrete, a mix where the aggregate is all recycled and the cement is replaced by up to 30 per cent of pulverized fly ash (PFA), which is basically the stuff that comes out of the back of coal-fired power stations.

You might argue that replacing just 30 per cent of Britain's cement with waste rubbish is about as helpful to the environment as forsaking a Range Rover Sport for a bicycle for just two and a half days a week. My point is that it's a start. And it gets better, because the cement company Cemex makes a product that contains 50 per cent Portland cement and 50 per cent ground granulated blast furnace slag (GGBS), another waste product from the iron smelting industry. It consumes only a fifth of the energy that cement uses to convert into a useable product. It produces only a tenth of the CO_2.

PFA and GGBS both work as cement replacements or enhancers and you might expect them to behave as poor relations. It's true that they take a few days longer to set, but when added to cement they make concretes that are much harder, more elastic, more waterproof, lighter in colour, more resistant to chemical damage (a common failing in concrete structures), more protective of the steel reinforcing rods and much less likely to crack or craze. New mixes being trialled in Australia now contain no cement at all.

STORE HEAT IN YOUR WINDOWS

In 2007 I built a house in a week. Admittedly I had help from 27 builders and experts, but the mission was to create a near-to-zero-carbon home in the course of five working days at the Grand Designs Live exhibition at ExCel in London. The finished two-bedroom home was constructed from Modcell panels on the ground floor; these are timber-framed wall sections pre-filled with straw bales and ready rendered. Upstairs was built from laser-formed Facit timber panels. For thermal mass we incorporated a window full of what looked like Vaseline – Aerogel, which melts and solidifies, absorbing and releasing the sun's energy as it does so. It works, but it makes the view through the window dull most of the time, as the material is opaque in its solid state. It would be so much easier if they'd filled the double-glazed unit with something that was cheaper and transparent.

Like, ooh, water. Which is exactly what the firm EEBT (Energy Efficient Building Technologies) has done.

Water has a very long, lazy thermal lapse. It takes for ever to heat up, which is why the sea is at its warmest around Britain's coast in September. In fact, it's the difference in thermal mass between land and sea that accounts for weather. The sea absorbs more heat than the land, from which, instead, warmed air rises. Cooler air from above the sea is sucked in to replace said rising warm air, bringing moisture/clouds. So EEBT has made thick double-glazed large bricks a few inches thick, filled with water. The water warms in the sun, absorbing heat that would otherwise perhaps overheat a room, only to release that heat in the evening. The only problem I can foresee with this system is if you go away for Christmas and turn the heating off, chances are you might return to find an ice wall.

LEFT: Timbrel vaulting at Crossway, near Stapleford, Kent, one of the UK's first carbon-neutral houses

BUILD OUT OF CANNABIS

If you're building from new and not underground, consider using Hemcrete instead of concrete. Hemcrete performs both as an insulant and as a thermal mass. And hemp locks up carbon as it grows. So your walls become a carbon sink as well as a heat sink.

DON'T RUSH TO CONDEMN CONCRETE IN FAVOUR OF LIME

Lime is elastic, it's breathable, it's the domain of the artisan builder. It is batch produced in small friendly kilns by elves. And it absorbs CO_2 during its lifetime, making it as planet friendly as a tree. So runs the argument.

But it seems that lime, although a noble material for authentic repair work to historic buildings (cement is only 200 years old; lime has been around for millennia), is not the clean, green building material we thought it was. In 2007 I wanted to find out about the environmental impact of lime production for an article I was writing. Eventually, I found an expert, Paul Livesey, chair of the British Standards Institute committee for cements and building lime. His research, published in a report, 'Reducing the Carbon Footprint of Masonry Mortar', exploded a number of myths. Yes, lime is batch produced in small quantities, but that process often makes it far more fuel hungry and less efficient than large-scale cement manufacturing; yes, lime absorbs large quantities of carbon dioxide as it undergoes the slow change from calcium hydroxide to calcium carbonate once in a structure, but (get this) it turns out that cement does too, absorbing most of the CO_2 chemically produced in its manufacture over a 50–60-year period (it's slower than lime but hey, concrete structures tend to hang around); yes, lime's carbon footprint can be lower than that of cement, but the best cement production facilities, incorporating fly ash or slag as cement replacements, can rival that footprint.

SUPER-CONCRETE

Right now, in Cambridge laboratories, in Australian research institutes and on a building site in Derbyshire, engineers and scientists are dicing with the very atomic structure of things like soil and figuring out how to make concrete without cement. The house that I built exploited the aggregating effect of clay mixed with soil and stone under pressure. The Italians have already demonstrated that cements made with crushed magnesium carbonate are CO_2 hungry, like lime mortars. An aerospace engineer I met in Derbyshire is formulating his own compacted mixture that he's branding as 'Dumblecrete'. So expect to find this – and 'soilcrete', 'mudcrete' and 'earthcrete' – in a hole in the ground near you, soon.

Chapter Three

HOW TO RECYCLE ENERGY

How many tyres do you think the British throw away every year? A few hundred thousand? Half a million? Try a staggering 48 million. They must be everywhere. I know for a fact that at least three of them are in my garage. Tyres are built in complex layers of steel and fabric webbing, interwoven with a chemical cocktail of latex and synthetic rubber that has been mixed with soot and cooked with sulphur in a process called vulcanization. It sounds demonic and it is, because the resultant tough rubber is no longer reversible. It can never be latex again. Just an ex-tyre.

So far, the ex-tyre industry has made a lot of money by selling around 86,000 tonnes a year to energy and cement companies, who burn the tyres as a fuel (and there are plenty of reports criticizing this activity for its public health implications). That accounts for around 17.5 per cent of the total. A further 18 per cent are reused (presumably in countries where people don't need to stop very quickly), just 12 per cent are retreaded, 12 per cent used to go to landfill but now are being strategically left in hedgerows, 7 per cent aren't even recovered, having been unstrategically left in hedgerows presumably, and just 33 per cent, a third, are recycled.

Into what? you might ask. Into all kinds of useful, human-friendly products, I might reply. Like children's toys and manbags skilfully sculpted from old inner tubes. Or rubbery covers on recycled notebooks. Or fake slate roofing tiles. Between them, these products might account for around 10 tonnes of tyres. That's a whopping 0.002 per cent of the tyre mountain.

The bulk of what is recycled is granulated into maggoty little particles called rubber crumbs. These are used loose as surfaces in horsey arenas and welded together to make play matting and playground surfaces that keep the nation's 17-year-olds occupied for hours as they attempt to prise the stuff out of the ground and set fire to it. There have been experimental attempts to incorporate rubber crumb into road surfaces and into concrete as an aggregate substitute. Engineers are still wondering what to do with all this bouncy gravel. Since 2006 it has become illegal to dump not only tyres in landfill but also processed crumb. There is, within the recycling industry, a sense of panic about the vast quantities of this material.

What's more, the proposed solutions for dealing with the vast majority of old tyres are crude and inefficient. They're examples not of recycling but of downcycling. And we need to be much more creative and devise as many opportunities to 'upcycle' products into new and noble uses, not base and mean ones. The tyre industry has responded intelligently by redesigning tyre compounds so that they last longer in the first place; retreading of tyres is also on the up. But these initiatives are paltry and the industry needs to improve its sustainability credentials dramatically. If you look just at the UK's figures, the fact remains that two-thirds of all waste tyres – that's 324,000 tonnes – ought to be sensibly and intelligently reused.

Given the amount of energy and effort that goes into making a tyre, it's reasonable that we should apply ourselves to reusing tyres and therefore reusing all that energy. So here are some other clever recycling principles that save energy.

BUILD YOUR HOUSE OUT OF CANNABIS

I'm serious about this. *Cannabis sativa* is not as strong as it used to be, at least not in its psychoactive sense. It has been genetically modified into a harmless form, but one that is just as physically strong. Farmers can once again grow hemp (its agricultural name) for all kinds of useful purposes, not least building houses.

Hemp grows fast. It is in fact the second fastest growing crop on the planet, after bamboo, so it can be slotted in between other crops during a growing season. It also requires almost no inputs and enriches the soil. Traditionally it was grown for rope-making because, as a tall crop, the tough fibres would reach 2 metres in length. It has also been used for paper-making, for fabrics and for carpeting. And for the door panels of the BMW 5 series.

The paper on which the American Declaration of Independence was drafted was made of hemp and in 1941 Ford produced a car that was 70 per cent manufactured from hemp plastic and built to run on hemp-sourced fuel. However, given that Ford modelled their prototype on the use of two banned US prohibition substances, hemp and alcohol, the idea didn't get very far.

All well and good in the pursuit of alternatives to cotton and polyester and whatever BMW door panels used to be made from. But I'm interested in the use of hemp shriv, the woody pulp that's left over once the fibres have been extracted and which until now has seen service only as horse bedding. When mixed with a binder such as building lime, this waste product can become Hemcrete, a walling material that can be sprayed, shuttered and cast like concrete. Hemcrete has a reasonable thermal mass and a reasonable insulative value too, rather like solid timber. And like solid timber it can lock large quantities of atmospheric carbon dioxide, absorbed during the growing cycle of the plant, into a building's structure, effectively making the structure carbon positive. The average hemp house can stow away about 20 tonnes of CO_2 into its walls this way, about 40 kilograms for every square metre of wall in comparison with a traditional brick, block and cavity wall, which is responsible for the production of about 100 kilograms of CO_2 for every square metre.

These characteristics make it a compelling technology. Its carbon credentials and minimal environmental impact, added to the fact that it is non-combustible, breathable, tough and flexible, make it an irresistible choice. And I like the way it recycles solar energy directly into the walls of a building, which would otherwise require significant amounts of fossil fuel to make them.

OR BUILD YOUR HOUSE OUT OF TYRES

It's possible to stick several thousand tyres into the walls of a building. To consolidate the tyres it's important that they are rammed full with earth and plastered over with lime or clay, so that the tyres disappear completely. Ramming is the hard bit: to turn a tyre into a giant brick requires that each one is pounded with earth in situ, in the wall. I have stood atop a 4-metre wall of tyres and tried this, and can attest that it requires balance, a 14-pound lump hammer and a lot of sweat. It is not an easy job – in fact it's back-breaking – but when rammed with earth until it is tight, rounded and too heavy to lift, a tyre in a wall is a beautiful thing, like a giant immovable brick, which provides immense thermal mass and structural stability. The only problem I can see with this form of construction is the time it takes to pound one tyre: 30 minutes of extreme cardio activity. Frankly the person who invents a quick, machine-aided method for ramming a car tyre in situ should get it patented, because once the time/effort problem has been sorted developers will be rushing to build rubber houses. I will, of course, immediately offer to buy the patent from them.

BUY TYRE CARPET

I don't mean the rubber-crumb underlay underneath your Wilton (which is, yes, made from old tyres) but the carpet itself, to wit Tirex. Tirex carpet tiles are made by slicing old tyres and rubber machinery belts into long French fries and then bonding them together side on. The durable fabric webbing inside the tyre wall is exposed as the top surface of the carpet, alternating with stripes of rubber, between which it's sandwiched. The resulting texture is a delight. The long striated patterns give the product the air of designer matting. The surface, not surprisingly, is supremely durable – so durable in fact that the manufacturers, Interface Flor, sell it as 'entrance matting'; and the stuff is resistant to all kinds of things like chemicals and dog sick. But most exciting of all is that Tirex doesn't look anything like a tyre. Its colours are grey and brown. Aesthetically it's a million miles away from rubber-crumb play matting. It is elegant and sophisticated, and every office in the world and quite a few homes ought to be carpeted with it.

CUT OUT THE FOSSIL-FUEL MIDDLE MAN AND GO STRAIGHT TO SOURCE

Let's be clear about this. All fuels are solar. They start in the sun. Even nuclear fuels mimic the weird atomic behaviour of stars as they burn hydrogen and turn it into helium – as I understand it. Meanwhile the precious petrol in your car's fuel tank, the gas that pops out of your hob, the coal in your power station, the oil squirted into your boiler – all are solar fuels. They're the super-condensed remains of trees that fell over hundreds of millions of years ago into a bog, trapping all that energy which the sun provided to help the tree grow in the first place. The fact that most of our fossil fuels are super-condensed and fluid makes them easy to transport, pump, store and use.

But you might consider timber as your fuel for your home. After all, your house doesn't go anywhere. If you live outside a smokeless zone and have access to some woodland, timber suddenly starts looking like an attractive proposition. For a start it can often be very cheap.

You find yourself happily less dependent on the outside world for your warmth and comfort. The very process of growing trees on an acre or two of land is immensely pleasurable. And the joys of heating or cooking with wood, the smell and sight of the flames for example, are a revelation.

Of course it can also be dirty and primitive. If you choose to install an open hearth in the middle of your home and burn wood as they did in Saxon huts, you'll smoke your family out and probably set fire to where you live. But technology is on your side here. How do I know? Because I am, at once, primitive woodland man and modern geeky gadget man. And I heat my home with a mixture of wooden fuels. As I explained earlier, the house has three woodburners for heating, each of which radiates heat rather than sending it up the chimney, and each of which can be locked down so that the fuel just glows gently overnight. I've also been experimenting with a timber-powered Rayburn which needs to be left on most of the time. It takes 40 minutes to reach super-hot temperatures, ideal for cooking Yorkshire pudding, and consumes a meagre stick or two every hour. It is absurdly efficient when compared to the woodburners.

And the best bit about burning wood is that it doesn't count. If you can source your timber from a renewable woodland nearby, or your hedgerow, or if your woodchip is recycled gash, you are pretty well carbon-neutral. The net carbon emissions from wood and local charcoal are near zero because 1) the timber would rot and release carbon into the atmosphere anyway and 2) more coppice growth or new planting will, if a woodland is properly managed, replace the timber you've cut to use.

But it is not always a virtuous circle. In deciding whether to install a woodchip or wood-pellet burner I opted for the former. Woodchip happens to be available where

I live from two suppliers, whereas pelleted wood, made from sawdust, would have to travel to get to me. I was particularly turned off when shown a packet of wood pellets from the Baltic states. This is a product that is widely available in Europe and which, despite being made from manufacturing waste, has had to travel a good few hundred miles before it's set on fire. And then I was told that the pellets originated from trees grown in the fallout plume of the Chernobyl disaster. Nice. This wasn't eco-friendly biomass they were selling: it was nuclear fuel.

66 All fuels are solar. They start in the sun. Even nuclear fuels mimic the weird atomic behaviour of stars 99

Chapter Four

HOME-MADE ENERGY

On average, every square metre of land on this planet soaks up about 250 watts of energy from the sun. On hot sunny days it can be a kilowatt. Not surprisingly, Spain is one of the biggest investors in solar and it has two of the world's largest solar 'power stations', while countries like China and the USA are not far behind. In these places the payback on solar-generated power is sensible.

If you stick a photovoltaic panel on your roof you're likely to recoup the cost in a few years. In the UK it's more like half a century. Whereas if you choose to stick a solar panel on your roof to do the rather mundane job of heating your hot water – by simply passing a fluid through some vacuum tubes or even just painting a radiator black and circulating your domestic hot water through it – you can recoup the cost (say around £3,500) in 7–15 years and you're even pre-heating that water in winter. The general consensus is that solar energy panels (photovoltaics that produce electricity) are expensive but that installing solar thermal (for hot water) is a no-brainer. Which is why governments pay us subsidies to install photovoltaics and in many countries (the US, UK and Germany, for example) insist that power companies buy the electricity back from us.

JOINED-UP THINKING

Ten years ago I climbed to the top of Jodrell Bank Radio Telescope to look at the electronics at the very focus of that giant dish – the focus being the tip of the pointy bit in the middle. The dish bounces extraordinarily faint electromagnetic signals from the far edge of the universe and concentrates them at the focus, where a collector responds to these ethereal vibrations and turns them into exciting bleeps for astronomers to coo over. The interesting thing for me was to discover that the electronics of the collector are kept at just below an unbelievably cool minus 272°C, a fraction of a degree off absolute zero, just to calm the electrons in the cables and circuits so that there is minimum interference from the electronics and the intergalactic signals can be perceived.

My point?

Electronics produce heat as they work (think of your computer or laptop) but they're only efficient when they're running cool, when energy isn't wasted as electrons bounce around. The great irony is that photovoltaic panels only really get going and start earning their keep when the sun comes out. When it gets warm, in fact. The sun's heat stimulates the electronics, which produce even more heat as they go to work, which immediately sticks the brakes on because the electronics start to become very inefficient. It's the catch-22 in the world of silicon circuitry.

In the years since Becquerel used selenium to experiment with photovoltaics in 1836, and Horace de Saussure captured solar heat in his homemade 'hotbox' in 1767, the two disciplines of using solar energy to produce either electricity or hot water have remained more

or less separate. Until a very short while ago, when a team of brilliant German physicists had the idea of putting the two technologies together.

At last. Their solution, one which I wish I'd thought of years ago, was to circulate the magic water from solar thermal panels around the electronics in solar photovoltaic panels providing – bingo! – two benefits: hotter water quicker from busy electronics that buzz away and produce waste heat and electronics which are cooled in the process. The result is the PV-T panel from a firm called Newform energy, which produces electricity at 25 per cent more efficiency than a standard photovoltaic panel.

Look out for PV-T hybrid heat pumps – the next generation of heat pumps, hooked up to PV-T panels for year-round total-solar space heating and hot water.

FIGURE OUT WHAT YOU'RE GOOD FOR

The one big thing to remember about sustainable living – in comparison with how we've grown accustomed to living in the 20th century – is that it is very specific to where it is. You can put a concrete and glass box anywhere on the planet, facing any direction, and as long as you pump enough energy into it (through heating and cooling) you can make a comfortable environment for human beings. Sustainable architecture is a bit less one-size-fits-all and a bit more contextual. It looks at what's available in a place. If your house is next to a waterfall, chances are a water turbine will be a good bet. Where I live, wind, rain and fog are the prescribed meteorology. If you live on a farm, then a biomass boiler burning your own woodchip is going to be far more sensible and less annoying to your neighbours than it would be if you lived in a city street.

Just to make sure you do the appropriate thing and fit the technology that's right for you, it's worth talking to a consultant. Not a salesman for one particular technology but someone who advises across – or sells – a host of different systems. If your home is good for wind and sun, then you can even buy a test kit that'll run for several months and produce data that can be analysed. I tried a Power Predictor, which is a little wind station complete with a wind vane and an anenometer that whizzes round in the breeze. I put it up 20 feet off the ground on a bracket attached to the gutter on one of the barns and each of its little cups spin and overflow, producing information about time, speed and direction that gets stored on an SD card, together with information from a solar sensor that measures the potential for solar panels. This should all determine whether my farm is a good site for panels and/or a small wind turbine. You know the kind: small enough to power a farm with, say, 12 kilowatts, large enough to cause a planning crisis on the parish council.

The alternative is to convert the Power Predictor itself into a mini-turbine. That would produce enough energy to power my watch.

PUT A JET ENGINE IN YOUR KITCHEN

Installing a gas turbine in your home may sound vaguely dangerous, but in my view it is a lot safer than driving at high speed while sitting on a 20-gallon container of highly volatile petroleum.

So why not install a gas power station on your kitchen wall that generates electricity and heats the home as a by-product?

The big thing in home energy production is now the boiler that thinks it's a power station, apparently. Combined heat and power (CHP) has been around for a while, not least because standard production of electricity in big power stations, from burning coal, oil, gas or from rubbing atoms together, generates large quantities of heat as a by-product. So small-scale CHP plants are sometimes used on flagship eco-projects or in tower blocks, burning biomass, for example, to generate electricity for domestic use and hot water for heating. On really thermally efficient projects where the buildings don't require much heat this can be a problem, because there's just too much heat produced as a by-product of the electricity generation. So in the more intelligent examples this heat is conducted away in an underground heat main to warm older homes that aren't as thermally efficient.

This all sounds pretty joined up and sensible. Far more sensible than the method of electricity production used by major power companies. They dump the heat from their generating plants in cooling towers. Then they transport electrons hundreds of miles across the grid, losing 6.5 per cent of the energy they produce in the process, thanks to the resistance of the cables and the distances travelled (this is a 2007 figure for the USA). So why not install a gas power station on your kitchen wall that generates electricity and heats the home as a by-product? Gas is a relatively clean fossil fuel and grid losses are around 1–2 per cent.

The sustainable energy guru and Cambridge professor David Mackay thinks installing hundreds of thousands of efficient gas turbine boilers in our homes is a mistake. In the highly influential *Sustainable Energy – Without the Hot Air* he writes:

'What the numbers actually show is that centralized electricity has many benefits in both economic and energy terms. Only in large buildings is there any benefit to local generation, and usually that benefit is only about 10 per cent or 20 per cent ... I think that growth of gas-powered combined heat and power would be a mistake. Such combined heat and power is not green: it uses fossil fuel and it locks us into continued use of fossil fuel. Given that heat pumps are a better technology, I believe we should leap-frog over gas-powered combined heat and power and go directly for heat pumps.'

Chapter Five

HOW TO NOT BURN ENERGY

In 2009 I launched the Great British Refurb, a campaign to save energy by refurbishing and 'retrofitting' our 26 million homes in the UK (which are responsible for around 27 per cent of our country's carbon emissions) to low-carbon standards. In order to meet the UK's target of reducing its carbon emissions by 80 per cent before 2050 we need to meet significant milestone targets by 2020 and every decade beyond. It is important to achieve CO_2 reductions in our day-to-day activities that can make a big dent on a sliding scale of carbon-saving.

The initiative was a combined effort, bringing together the Energy Savings Trust, *Grand Designs*, WWF and the Green Building Council, plus retailers and politicians from all parties. It requires a combined effort, because the figures are daunting. Most of the housing stock that will be around in 2050 already exists, so any flashy eco-developments that we build from now on, though important, cannot change energy consumption significantly. By 2020 we need to be refurbishing at least 1.6 million homes a year. It is a mighty task, but one not beyond the capabilities of our now-dormant construction industry, nor our design professions.

Britain's older housing is immensely varied. We can't just slap insulation board over every home in the country and then apply a coat of efficient German render. We need carefully tailored solutions from a re-energized construction industry. We need an army of properly accredited and trained installers and the involvement of surveyors and architects as local consultants. I'd like to see communities come together to empower themselves as clients and for government to provide local grant aid.

And I'd like to see energy companies becoming the financiers of all of this. Our homes are pretty efficient machines for warming the planet right now, but if we can retrofit them on the scale we need to, then our collective energy consumption will tumble. This idea is already re-orientating the power companies. In discussing turbines and photovoltaics I have already mentioned how these firms are having to turn into energy management businesses, buying and selling electricity. From here it's a short hop to financing energy use, so at the Great British Refurb, we've undertaken some research and explored the feeling among the financial institutions for this idea. It turns out there is an appetite for a model where:

1. Your energy company pays, say, £15,000 to retrofit your home with energy-saving technologies and measures.

2. The savings are immediate and cut your energy consumption to a fraction.

3. However, you carry on paying an energy bill – which is modestly reduced – as, effectively, a mortgage or loan.

This way, the energy company has a new revenue stream; financial institutions lend to those companies knowing that the investment is securely spread across millions of homes; you get reduced bills and a much more comfortable home, and your property is upgraded in quality and value – for free. I find the idea irresistible. Meantime, here are some of the 'no-brainers' the Great British Refurb promotes.

Avoid being seduced by the trinkets and gadgets of domestic life. A glass and steel balustrade may seem exciting but a good, plasterboarded, simple low wall is much cheaper and more of a piece with the building as a whole. The real pleasure of a properly designed house lies in the arrangement of the components, not decoration.

PROOF YOUR DRAUGHTS

At home I used a combination of about six different self-adhesive draught-excluding rubber strips around the doors and windows of my old house. The effect was immediate and so noticeable I had to take my third pullover off. Fill gaps under skirting boards with newspaper softened in water. Fit keyhole covers and a brush cover over your letterbox. Draught excluding is the easiest measure you can take. Don't do this and you're spending money on heating the atmosphere outside your home.

DOUBLE – OR TRIPLE YOUR GLAZING

If you haven't got double glazing, then at least put in secondary glazing—a second frame of glass behind the first. It's a cheap solution. I've been experimenting with see-through insulating shutters. These are glass double-glazing units fixed into a set of thin, engineered timber frames hinged together.

TURN DOWN THE BOILER

This is the cheapest thing you can do. You won't notice the difference by lowering the thermostat temperature by one degree. Additionally, conserve heat in the heating system by properly insulating your hot-water cylinder (some new brands come already super-insulated) and fitting thermostatic valves to radiators, preventing rooms from overheating.

GIVE YOUR HOUSE A HAT

Check your loft insulation. Whatever you've got, double it – or triple it! Heat rises and then dissipates through our buildings' roofs, so two or three layers of insulating fleece will slow that process right down. There are new brands of fleece made from polyester, recycled from plastic bottles. I like to use sheep's wool insulation from firms like Black Mountain because it breathes and can regulate the moisture content in a timber roof. And it's from British sheep. But if you live in Australia or New Zealand you may choose to insulate your attic with possum fur or merino wool respectively.

FILL THE VOIDS IN YOUR WALLS

Cavity insulation is one of the most significant measures you can take, because about 40 per cent of lost heat in a poorly performing house goes through the walls. In a house with average gas needs, cavity insulation will save 42 per cent off your gas bill. The cost of cavity filling the walls of a three-bedroom house at £250 will give an annual saving thereafter, every year, of £176 (at 2006 prices).

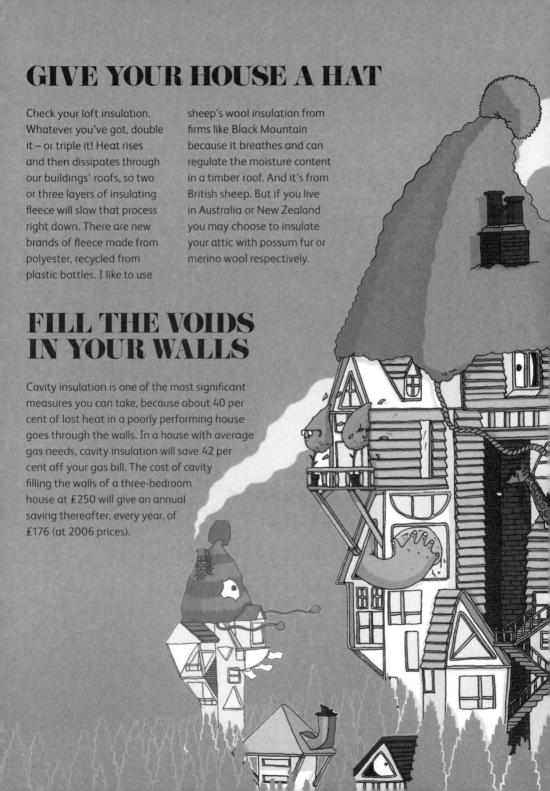

BUY GREEN ENERGY
IN THE FIRST PLACE

Buying energy from a green supplier can cut your carbon footprint and reduce the overall fossil fuel energy for which you're responsible. Some suppliers use their profits to invest in green technologies but buy and distribute power from the big companies. Others build their own wind turbines or solar parks or buy only from renewable sources. Prices are often comparable to those of the big power companies, but importantly these companies know that they're going to be selling power to ethically minded customers who are probably going to be doing their best to cut consumption anyway. In other words, making the switch to a green power company will more than likely form part of a wider change you make in your energy consumption patterns. So even if the electricity costs a bit more for every kilowatt hour, you'll probably be saving money anyway. Which makes it a no-brainer.

UPGRADE YOUR
HEATING SYSTEM

If your boiler is old, then all it does is burn fuel and get hot. Newer models – known as 'condensing boilers' – have a secondary heat exchanger in the outlet flue that absorbs heat from the hot gases that leave the combustion chamber. If you're not going to install a biomass woodchip burner or other renewables, at the very least replace your old boiler with a condensing version. It will not save the planet or humanity, but it is a modest start.

UNPLUG

Domestic appliances on standby are responsible for about 8 per cent of residential electricity demand.

At home, I'm helped in my efforts to turn everything off in the first place by a little remote control that switches appliances off for me by wirelessly linking to three socket adaptors in a room. It's got buttons on it that I can understand, marked with words like 'on' and 'off', and it means that I can remotely turn the TV, the stereo and the table lamps all on and off at the mains, saving pounds without leaving the sofa. All this will, of course, happen automatically in the future. Houses will be built with software that monitors the energy performance of the building and its consumption and power-manages power-hungry appliances like televisions and tumble dryers. I know this because I'm already building those houses.

Meantime, it's clear that achieving meaningful power savings with our appliances means unplugging them all at the mains – difficult when some, such as satellite TV boxes, guzzle standby power and refuse to function if regularly powered down.

SHUT UP

Work I've been doing with some of Britain's top environmental engineers suggests that even a poorly fitting timber shutter offers you the same performance as good double glazing. It'll improve your home security too. I've made my own from oak-veneered plywood. Thick curtains also offer fantastic insulation.

INSULATE YOUR WALLS

Many houses do not have cavity walls. However, companies such as the insulation firm Knauf have developed systems to insulate walls either on the exterior of a building or within the existing interior walls. The exterior systems extol the virtues of cladding the building with blocks of plastic foam, rendering them with a flexible acrylic coating. They also create tricky technical challenges: roof eaves usually need extending to project over the new tubby walls; drains and downpipes need moving and window reveals require remodelling. And their approach is to plastic wrap a building, perhaps trapping in moisture and certainly covering up the original materials of the house – materials which may have a local or historical charm.

So if you really do intend to insulate your building on the outside, go for a system that uses wood-pulp fibreboard or Hereklith board as an insulating substrate, and breathable lime mortar as a finish. And be prepared to suffer the wrath of your neighbours.

The interior systems get my vote. Like the exterior systems, I've seen them being used, only to find any suspicions I've had about them evaporate. I had thought that in a period home with features and traditional detailing, cladding an interior wall with insulation would utterly obscure most of them. In fact, given that a huge number of homes are terraced or have party walls, this often means that only the front and back walls need to be treated – and in a Great British Refurb project we ran in Manchester, skirting boards, window reveals, dado rails and picture rails were first carefully removed and then planted back on to the wall's new, insulated internal skin. I had thought that damp might build up within the new construction, but it turned out that all the materials were highly breathable, there being no need for waterproof plastics on the inside of the building. I had thought that the intervention into the homeowners' lives would be intolerable, but in fact the process of insulating the front and back walls to the house, lagging pipes and insulating the attic and cellar space took just a few days with minimal disruption. The website greatbritishrefurb.co.uk has details.

We also ran a GBR project in Bristol where the owners are now energy positive – the home is so well insulated and the photovoltaic panels so effective that they're selling electricity to the Grid and making a profit!

CHECK YOUR BOTTOM

If your home has a cellar, get down there and insulate up between the joists of the ground floor. Use hemp or wool batts of insulation, which will stay put once in place and breathe, allowing the timbers of the floor to remain moisture free. Both hemp and wool are hygroscopic, which means they can absorb and hold large amounts of moisture without it affecting their thermal performance. This is why whenever out walking in the mountains you should always wear wool not cotton clothes. Or hemp jeans, I suppose, since jeans were originally made from hemp.

FIT INSULATED BLINDS

Heatsaver, an American firm with branches worldwide, makes insulated blinds from the multilayer thin insulation sold for roofspaces. This looks like the covering of a NASA spaceship, and has up to 14 gossamer strata of foam and reflective plastic foil. Heatsaver uses a less complex structure in its product, which has the appearance of interlined cream linen Roman blinds. Its secret, however, lies in a specially designed channel on the wall, in which the blind slides.

BUY POWER-MEASLY APPLIANCES

This can make an enormous difference to your energy bill. A typical household might get through 3,700 kilowatt hours of electricity every year, assuming gas heating. Lighting will gobble 750kWh. The rest goes on machinery of one kind or another.

To reduce that, we need to buy 'A'-rated appliances. An 'A'-rated washing machine of the highest efficiency might consume half the energy and half the water of one eight years old. Its spin cycle might leave clothes with 25 per cent less water in them (and if you're drying in a tumble dryer or in a heated house that's 25 per cent less energy needed further down the laundry line). A very few washing machines even come with a connection pipe to your hot tap as well as your cold (this is a much more efficient way of heating the water). This is just one example of how, with a bit of forethought and research, you can slash the carbon footprint of your home.

And there is one fundamental point to make about any machine a human being uses, be it a Range Rover, tumble dryer or laptop. What determines its true ecological value and carbon footprint is not the label, or the manufacturer, but you and me. How we use machines makes the biggest difference of all. Just as I could drive a Range Rover to the shops, so I could also cycle or walk. I could in fact cycle or walk so much that I fill my Range Rover up with petrol just once a month. So it is with kettles, which we all constantly overfill. And washing machines, which on average we underfill with clothes. And dishwashers, which are never loaded to capacity. A German study comparing the energy intensity of making, buying and using a dishwasher compared with washing up by hand had the dishwasher win hands down. But only if it was loaded fully every time.

INSTALL LED LIGHTING AND RETROFIT COMPACT FLUORESCENTS

The governments of the Western world have embarked on a campaign to ban the old-fashioned light bulb. Sales of higher-wattage conventional tungsten light bulbs are already being phased out. This is because although tungsten lighting is warm and beautiful and we all like it, it is also inefficient and works marginally better at heating a room than it does lighting it. So goodbye old-fashioned, evil, planet-warming light bulbs on which you could fry an egg.

Hello instead to the new-fangled world of compact fluorescent and LEDs, which barely produce enough heat to hatch an egg. We're all familiar with both these technologies now. Fluorescent lighting was invented in 1901 and LEDs came into the world in the mid-1920s. Fluorescent lighting is associated with offices and Russian housing projects; LEDs (short for Looks Extremely Dim!) are familiar from electrical equipment and the side lights of any modern Audi. Both are extensively used in submarines. It is also fair to say that neither has won the hearts or minds of the average householder. But that is changing now that both technologies are getting cheaper, brighter and warmer in colour.

When it comes to performance – how much light a diode or compact fluoro will produce as against an old-fashioned bulb – we must delve further into the mysterious language of lighting. I'm sorry about this, but I consider it a matter of principle that you know about these things so that you can feel empowered in your local DIY store, understand the labels and make decisions that don't turn out to be mistakes. I want to help.

The efficiency of every kind of light source can be measured. A 60-watt tungsten bulb will produce around 850 lumens. A lumen is a quantified thingy of light. For every watt of electricity that the bulb gobbles it therefore blares out a whole 14 lumens. A compact fluorescent generates less heat and more light and generally produces around 50 or 60 lumens per watt of electricity, making it much more efficient. It's just like miles per gallon in your car.

But the LED electric car is accelerating fast down the motorway and about to undertake the compact fluoro-mobile on the inside lane.

The Cree LR6 downlighter now produces 650 lumens at 54 lumens per watt. Ultraleds sells a retrofit 12-volt lamp that replaces a 45-watt downlighter bulb with the same output (350 lumens) but consuming a tenth of the energy, and Photonstar produces a range of warm and cool white surface-mounted and recessed spots with a similar kind of efficiency.

Meanwhile researchers in Turkey have got a whopping 300 lumens out of one LED. That's bonkers. So RIP the incandescent light bulb. By getting rid of it we can currently cut the carbon impact of domestic lighting by about 75 per cent. Soon, we'll be able to save even more. With 9 million tonnes of CO_2 every year in Britain attributable to lighting that can make a significant difference in moving towards a low-carbon economy. In saying goodbye to the old-fashioned light bulb we need to embrace the LED. Glowingly.

Cree LR6 six-inch LED downlights in a kitchen on the island of Oahu, Hawaii

Chapter Six
STORING ENERGY AT HOME

Among the myriad ways in which energy can be stored, the chemical battery is the most familiar and obvious. The car – and now the heavy lithium-ion hybrid electric car – seems like the natural home for large batteries, not our houses. Yet the very walls of our homes can behave like big batteries, sucking in the sun's thermal energy and storing it to be slowly released once the sun has set. That's thermal mass at work.

By playing around with different heavy materials like stone, earth, concrete and water, it's possible to play with the thermal mass of a building and the land around it as though it were a giant heat battery.

The other not-so-well-known physics phenomenon that it's possible to play around with is latent heat, which finds its expression in buildings in phase-change materials. These sound as though they are the stuff that the next generation of Terminators are made of, or a new range of fashion fabrics, but they are in fact materials like liquids and gels (and even molten salts) that are especially good at handling latent heat. Of course the very words 'latent heat' are themselves enough to phase change anyone into a gel.

So, in order to explain these concepts let me ask whether (ladies) you have ever noticed when hairspraying your latest style into place that when using the can continuously for more than 15 minutes it gets extremely cold? Or whether (gentlemen) when gas welding steel you have observed ice forming around the nozzle of the gas canister? If not, I'm sure you've often noticed that when raiding the minibar in a hotel, the inside of the fridge is cold but the cupboard in which it sits is extremely hot.

This is all latent heat at work. And here's the most obvious example of all: the bactericide alcohol hand gel you find in hospitals and that you can buy at the pharmacy. Rub it on and it disappears, cooling your hands as it does so. This is because the molecules of hand gel (like all molecules) bounce around full of energy, happy to be hand-gel molecules. They collide a bit, they have room to play, they have fun, they occasionally mercilessly kill a bacterium or two. In the bottle they exist in a sort of liquid state – or phase – and if you were to freeze your hand gel bottle in your freezer, the liquid would change phase to a cold solid, in which the molecules would stand around shivering, tightly bunched in a smaller volume, unable to commit much bactericide. The energy they had as a liquid hasn't disappeared: it has simply changed in the freezing process from kinetic energy to heat, which was released during the freezing. That bit is the surprise. That molecular movement, kinetic energy, is released as heat when a liquid is cooled. Equally, as a frozen solid bottle of orange juice thaws out in your kitchen, it draws heat from

Skylight in a house in Peckham, London, engineered by Monty Ravenscroft and designed to avoid casting shade on the two adjacent nineteenth-century houses

the surrounding air to defrost the orange juice molecules and get them jumping around a bit. So much so that a layer of thin ice will often form on the outside of the bottle as heat is drawn through the glass wall to the juice.

So, in changing phases from gas to liquid or liquid to solid, a material will give off latent heat. In the reverse case, when passing from solid to liquid or liquid to gas, a material needs an extra boost of energy to make the molecules dance more: it needs latent heat, drawn usually from the environment around it. The gel absorbs heat from your hand, leaving it feeling cold, as it expands into a gas.

Ice-cream makers have known this principle for centuries. Before Mr Whippy vans, they would mix table salt with ice to liquefy it and so quickly draw off any vestigial heat from the surrounding area. This way they could super-cool metal containers and freeze blend their concoctions of eggs, milk and sugar. Nowadays we use fridges. The rattle of the rear end of a Mr Whippy is the sound of the wobbling compressor, the key working element of any fridge. It simply squashes a fluid in a pressurized system of tubes, to extract the latent heat from it by forcing the fluid to occupy a smaller physical space and jamming the molecules together. The heat leaks out of the back of the fridge; the compressed, colder fluid is then quickly released back to low-pressure freedom inside the body of the fridge, where it instantly absorbs heat from its surroundings – your packets of Froobs, your orange juice and your four-week-old leftover can of tuna – before being circulated outside the fridge and once again compressed. The whole miraculous cycle moves heat from one place to another.

So do fans and hot-water pipes, of course, but the clever thing about a compressor is its ability to suck heat out of one place and then transfer it specifically to another place in a concentrated form.

I should add that there is one example of latent-heat technology that we all intrinsically understand. One that a simply designed house with a vent at the top and some opening windows on the ground floor will exploit. Sweating. As your skin moisture evaporates in moving air it cools the skin. Simple. It turns out that the most efficient cooling systems of all are our own bodies.

ABOVE: A quick-build, carbon-positive Baufritz house, constructed from toxin-free natural materials

THERMAL MASS MATERIALS

You might well think that the golden rule of eco-construction is to bung in as much insulation as you can. But thermal mass is crucial both for storing heat and for regulating a building's temperature over the day/night cycle and the longer seasonal cycle as well. If your house is a lightweight timber construction with no heavy materials, there are a number of ways of improving its mass and slowing down its thermal 'lapse'. These techniques involve what are called 'phase changing materials'. The most high-tech is to use plasterboard or wet plaster that contains a BASF product called Micronal, made from petrochemical waxes. Micronal melts at between 18 and 23°C, absorbing latent heat to do so. As it cools in the evening it slowly solidifies and releases the same latent heat. Using 30mm of Knauf plasterboard with Micronal in it is equivalent to building a concrete internal skin inside your home 14 centimetres thick. I'm currently experimenting with lime plasters, Micronal and Hemcrete, to see if it's possible to apply a breathable, insulating thermal mass finish to walls in historic buildings.

If you have yet to insulate your home you could even, subject to approval from your local authority, consider waste wood wool (treated with borax as a human-friendly fire preventive). Wood has a surprisingly high thermal mass and Baufritz, the German ecological construction company, makes a point of not only constructing their houses but also insulating them entirely with timber.

EARTH WALLS

The water-window is an example of something called a trombe wall: a purpose-built heat sink somewhere in a building where passive solar energy can be collected and stored. In the house I built in 2007, we constructed the staircase around a 10-foot high trombe wall made from rammed earth: a tonne or two of clay, soil and stones that were pounded into some metal shuttering over two days using pneumatic hammers. The advantage was a wall formed with no binders or cement that was as tough as brick, as beautiful as an unearthed piece of archaeology and as useful as a night storage heater running for free. The disadvantage was having to put up with what sounded like two Harley-Davidsons revving all day on our building site.

HOW TO FIND HIDDEN ENERGY IN THE GROUND

Air conditioners move heat from buildings and dump it into the atmosphere. Ground-source heat pumps work like giant reverse fridges, sucking the stored heat of the sun from the ground in a series of pipes and compressing the latent heat out of those pipes inside buildings. Air-source heat pumps work like an air-conditioning unit backwards. We heat, cool, chill and freeze different parts of our environments using nothing but that Mr Whippy technology: phase-change fluids (which, like the hand gel, are often alcohol based), circulating pumps, compressors and the principle of latent heat.

The heat pump is the new stalwart machine of the home. Like the Toyota Prius which still drinks petrol as well as running on its own electricity, the heat pump still consumes electricity from the mains (up to 3 kilowatts for every 5 kilowatts it produces), making it a sort of variegated green product. It's not as simple – or as miserly to run – as solar panels that heat your water. Nor is it as brilliant as photovoltaic panels, which generate electricity from solar energy with no input from the grid.

The heat pump works just like a fridge, but backwards, sucking stored solar energy from the earth (not from the earth's core – that would be geo-thermal) via enormous lengths of fluid-filled coiled pipe buried 4 or 5 feet down. A condenser (which squeezes a liquid or gas) then exploits the principle of latent heat.

Heat pumps are the immediate future of heating not just new buildings but older ones too. The heat pump is the new boiler and we should favour these boilers over new miniature domestic gas boilers that generate both electricity and heat.

Not that we can irrefutably crown the heat pump as the heating technology of the next 50 years. Next up is a new generation of absorption chillers that use a more complicated combination of fluids. There's even talk of powering them entirely from the sun.

HOW TO HIDE ENERGY IN YOUR WALLS

I talked earlier about thermal mass and using heavy materials in construction for trapping heat from the sun – or from your logburner or electric-bar fire – to be released after dark. But there are clever, high-tech construction materials that swap the principle of thermal mass for that of phase change. They are clever latent-heat materials. And they know it, which makes them somewhat expensive.

BASF, the German chemical firm, are among the leaders in this field. One devious invention of theirs is Micronal, a white powder that is in fact made from tiny leak-proof capsules, each containing a minuscule amount of synthetic wax, similar to paraffin. This is a phase-change material that melts around the ambient temperature that human beings like – between 18 and 23°C – absorbing extra heat that we don't enjoy, from, say, a hot summer sun, only to slowly release that heat as it solidifies at night. Ingenious.

Du Pont meanwhile has its own paraffin-wax/Vaseline-type product that it incorporates into a sandwich construction board. This can sit in the cavity of a timber-framed building and act as a heat store, melting and solidifying to compensate for the daily cycle of warm and cold that any building experiences. Knauf Insulation even does a plasterboard with microcapsules of Micronal that do the same thing.

HOW TO HIDE ENERGY UNDER YOUR HOUSE

I recently visited a weirdly interesting house, full of ducts and pipes buried in its heavy concrete walls. This was a super-high thermal mass building, an experimental home in Kent built by an engineer, Paul Tarling, and his wife, Jo, for her parents. It was the last, the very last design of the late, great Richard Paxton, sideways thinker and architect of the next brilliant idea.

Paul was his services engineer, himself an ingenious inventor of solutions. So not surprisingly the house was constructed like a machine, built to make light of the vagaries of temperature fluctuations on this planet, fluctuations from night to day and winter to summer, by absorbing, storing and releasing heat and energy. Water tubes in the pre-tensioned curved concrete roof sections now help the building cool in summer; water is pumped through the roof as it becomes hotter in the sun, drawing heat away and circulating it through a ground-source heat pump,

sucking warmth out of the structure of the building and storing it via a network of tubes, underground, via in fact the building's pile foundations in the very earth beneath. In winter, the same heat pump works backwards, sucking the same heat out of the same ground, pushing it into the building.

Normally, ground-source heat pumps need large expanses of land in order to work. This is because the heat they draw in the winter is usually solar heat: heat that hits the ground, warms it up, keeps it warm (the earth at about a metre underground being more or less a constant 12°C) and sits there, waiting for hundreds of metres of buried plastic pipe filled with a fluid to collect it.

Paul and Jo's system is different, however. They didn't have an acre of land to dig up but a tiny site for this house, which is why they sank their tubes into their foundations. The ground-source heat pump doubles as a boiler and as air conditioning: they need the summer sun to help them put heat back into the ground in the warmer months. As Paul explained, 'The size of the plot is so small we had no option but to drill down and suck the heat from the earth underneath the building. But the sun doesn't shine there. We have to use our roof as a solar collector and put heat back in the summer because if we didn't, we'd just keep sucking heat out of the earth underneath us. We'd freeze the ground beneath us solid!'

66 **The size of the plot is so small we had no option but to drill down and suck the heat from the earth underneath the building. But the sun doesn't shine there.** 99

Laying the foundations for Paul and Jo Tarling's experimental home in Kent, designed by the late, great Richard Paxton

HOW TO HIDE
ENERGY IN THIN AIR

I can understand how the heat recovery unit works in my tumble dryer: cold dry air is drawn in and then gets passed over a series of flattened tubes that contain the warm damp air that's getting exhaled. The heat is transferred, saving the machine energy. I know it works because the air coming out of the machine isn't warm any longer, it's just room temperature. A heat recovery unit working in a house (it has to be an airtight one) works in just the same way and can, brilliantly, extract 95 per cent of waste heat from the stale air.

So if you're building a new home, don't install a boiler; instead design your house so that you can fit one of these. And pop an air-source heat pump on the back or a solar panel on your roof for good measure, to heat your water.

HOW TO HIDE ENERGY
SOMEWHERE ELSE

I installed a biomass boiler on my farm to run on waste scrap wood from chopped-up broken pallets. It heats five buildings and sits in a barn on a concrete plinth. Next to it I had to build a 90-cubic-metre chip store. And next to that a loading bay, so that the broken pallet company could just dump their product and scarper. And next to that a giant thermal buffer.

You might be forgiven for thinking that a thermal buffer is a big fluffy polishing cloth. In fact it is a big fluffy water tank that contains 10,000 litres. It's called a buffer because it sits in between the boiler and the buildings it's heating, both literally and technically. This is because old-fashioned oil boilers, the like of which I used to run, are lazy and like to burn gently all day. Wood boilers need to run at high temperatures to burn all the tars and gases in timber – too high a temperature for comfortably heating buildings and people. So the solution is to install a big insulated water tank that the boiler can heat in fiery short bursts and from which water can be drawn off and circulated around a heating system.

Other higher-tech systems use liquids like Vaseline or wax that melt and also absorb latent heat as well.

HOW TO HIDE ENERGY IN THE FRIDGE

There is a term in the energy industry that is much less catchy than 'phase change' or 'latent heat'. It's 'frequency adaptive power energy rescheduler'. Invented in the 1970s, FAPERs have yet to really catch on. In layman's terms you could call a FAPER a new kind of battery, an intelligent one at that; or rather, the clever electronics that can manage, read and make intelligent decisions about power and power management.

66 Our national grid is not a particularly intelligent beast. It rumbles away, burning any kind of fuel it can get its hands on... producing 57 gigawatts at peak demand 99

Our national grid is not a particularly intelligent beast. It rumbles away, burning any kind of fuel it can get its hands on (gas, coal, diesel, uranium), producing 57 gigawatts at peak demand, which is 57 billion watts. And it has to estimate what peak demand is going to be, despite us and our whims. The fact that we all like to put the kettle on in the ad break on TV, for example. At any one time the grid has to have

a certain amount of what's called 'spinning reserve'. This doesn't mean dormant or cold power stations ready to fire up when demand peaks in mid-winter (and they are ready); it doesn't even mean warmed-up power stations or turbines (it takes a good two hours to warm one up). It means stations that are burning fuel like billy-o and just wasting the steam, ready, at 20 seconds' notice, for that surge on the grid as we all make tea as One Nation.

But it turns out my fridge can not only drink energy but also store it and control it. The Grid may be dumb but my fridge could possibly be clever.

This is because you can easily see just how lax or how stressed the National Grid is by measuring the cycle rate of the alternating current (it's set at 50 hertz) at any plug socket in the country. With the right microprocessor, a fridge or freezer can do that. It can also switch itself off if it's able to realize it's already become cold enough. With millions of fridges in the UK (2.5 million are sold every year) we could liberate up to 1.9 gigawatts of electricity, at an instant, when needed. For every hour of our fridges' intelligent stewardship, we would prevent 950 tonnes of carbon dioxide being produced.

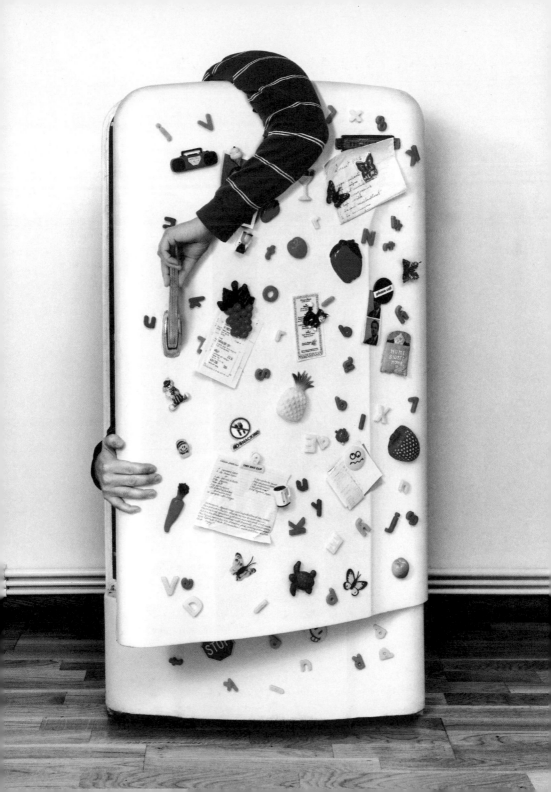

PART
TWO
BUILD

DINGS

Chapter Seven
MAKING A PLACE TO LIVE

There are places on the planet where energy is palpable. Standing next to the row of electricity generators in the turbine hall of the Hoover Dam on the Colorado river makes 4 billion kilowatt hours a year of energy really palpable. But what seems staggering still is the effort required to tame the forces of nature into delivering that energy: the construction of a 725-foot-high structure that contains over 3 million cubic metres of concrete and creates a lake 110 miles long.

Big numbers and big pieces of engineering, wrought by men, belong in the macho realm of the industrial age, a period that has lasted from the mid-19th century until now. Since we live in that world and enjoy the material benefits that things like 4 billion kWh of electricity can provide, it's hardly surprising that we are in thrall to such Great Engineering Wonders of the World. We live now in a time of super steel and colossal concrete, when to build highest, longest and fastest is what counts. Where the success and power of a project – be it a dam or a bridge or a new palm-tree-shaped island off the coast of Dubai – is measured no longer in human terms but by using a complex equation of diesel, machinery, raw materials, gas welding, political will and marketing. But mainly diesel, because it helps drive all the other factors. The human energy that goes into a project seems lost in this thicket, or at least subjugated.

But of course without human will and energy we'd all be living in caves and clubbing each other to death. Without inspiration and commitment and will, human beings achieve nothing. And that inspiration, that desire to get up every morning and improve our lot and our environment, while creating great things, also has effects: there is an environmental impact from altering the world and using resources (the Hoover Dam effectively stopped the downstream flow of the Colorado for six years, creating a saline delta that proved catastrophic for the biodiversity of a 40-mile stretch of river). There's also the positive social impact that comes from solving engineering challenges like generating power, bridging great distances and moving people about. And there are the cultural changes that come with the impressiveness of it all and the big contribution to the built environment that even a dam can make. Gordon B. Kaufmann, the British-born architect who designed the *Los Angeles Times* headquarters, lent a similarly massive Art Deco look to the Hoover Dam, with the result that the turbine hall, spillway, turrets and inlet towers are designed in the spirit of the age, adorned with the visual language of the Navajo and Pueblo people of the area (some of whom were no doubt displaced when their homesteads were inundated).

If you've ever tried to build a wall or saw a tree up or even plaster a room, you'll know how extraordinarily tiring and difficult these processes are. If you haven't, then I suggest you go out right now and try one of them. Skilled manual labour, the work of the artisan, should never be underestimated. Organized labour, where artisans are coordinated under some kind of master plan, is even more impressive.

ENERGY TO BUILD

PLANNING

We can ooh and aah at the Hoover Dam but its statistics are in the end still those of size and speed. It took only nine years to plan and five to build. The concentrated effort of the hundreds of individuals involved was spent in a decade or so, thanks to the assistance of fossil fuels. Meanwhile, Salisbury Cathedral required the efforts of generations of men to build it. The entire structure, built in one consistent Early English style, took over 100 years. It took another 60 to add the spire. So no one man can have claimed to be its architect or visionary. The energy to build such a gargantuan thing from stone over such a long period must have been infectious, zealous and passionate. Craftsmen would have dedicated their entire working life to this one building – which, compared to other European cathedrals, went up very, very quickly.

But there are quieter projects than the Hoover Dam or Salisbury Cathedral that can still make the soul sing. We marvel at a monastery clinging to a rock face in the Himalayas, for instance. It may well have been put there for reasons of remoteness and inaccessibility, but these reasons would have made it much more perilous to build. And it would have been built with wooden scaffolding and hand-made tools by men with wheelbarrows and rickety ladders and no diesel. Men of belief and commitment.

There is a place in central Rome where you can not only feel the human energy that has gone into building it but almost wallow in it. I'm not talking about the Roman Forum or the Colosseum, which are now broken piles of stone, and I'm not talking about the Vatican, which for the most part feels as though it was built by Titans for something other than human use. I mean the Campidoglio on the Capitoline Hill, a square designed by Michelangelo, a brilliantly manipulative piece of outdoors theatre and an exemplary piece of town planning.

We don't think of town planning as important, but it is more important than art and sculpture, more important than interior design, because it determines how our built environment is. We have a choice whether to go and look at a painting or a sculpture in a gallery. But walking down the street or travelling to work we have no choice at all about the buildings we have to look at and the roads and pavements we have to cross.

For millennia villages have grown up in quite haphazard ways and towns have needed walls, roads and assembly points for soldiers and police. As democracies grew, so towns and cities also needed meeting spaces and market places. The streets and agora spaces of Roman towns were regimented and organized in a grid-iron pattern, rational and ordered.

08

Our cities, like sedimentary organisms, accrete layers and layers of more stuff: roads, bypasses, flyovers, signage, extensions on buildings, dead spaces, new accidental green spaces. It takes a trained designer to come along and put it all in order again, sweep away the superfluous and polish up the stuff that's valuable but which has been neglected. That is context: stuff that has been overlooked or hidden but which has invaluable worth as a cultural map of the place.

PRINCIPLE

09

We have a choice whether to go and look at a painting or a sculpture in a gallery. Interior design is certainly a very private affair that doesn't concern most of us. We even, for the most part, still have choice as to what music we listen to. But walking down the street or travelling to work we have no choice at all about the buildings we have to look at and the roads and pavements we have to cross.

Our experience of architecture should improve, the closer we get to it. And for that matter the longer we use it.

DESIGN PROCESS

The process of design is something we all do, every day. It involves understanding a problem, researching around it, developing a number of solutions (based on training, experience and a bit of lateral thinking), testing those solutions (maybe by trying them out in the real world or as a model or just as an imagined mental process) and refining them down to one elegant solution – which itself can be tested again and again and maybe one day revised. If you've ever imagined how a car is designed, you'll probably feel at home with this description. But how on earth do we use design every day?

My answer is that you employ the design process when, for instance, you plan a menu for a dinner. You use your experience and interests, a knowledge of convention and taste, of individuals' preferences. You might work it out on paper, checking the ingredients you have or you know you can get. You might adventurously try cooking a dish you've never done before. And throughout – and afterwards – you'll reappraise what you've done to make it as good or better next time.

Throughout your day, when choosing which tie to wear or which route to take into town, you're using design. Design takes the creative, expressive side to human nature, the bit we enjoy letting off the leash, and subjects it to a rational process – which of itself can be enjoyable to employ. And what is the difference between you and the designer or you and the architect? Nothing. They're just trained to do it a hundred times faster than you with a thousand times more pieces of relevant information. Just to prove my point, the picture on the next page shows the design model used by NASA. Around the world you will find that design models are more or less the same, because the process has been refined over thousands of years. It is immensely pliable and responsive, and in my view its great strength lies in its ability to incorporate activities from both the left and the right sides of the brain.

So as we, the planet, stare blinkingly into a future of peak oil, climate change and massive cultural change as well, the designers among us are staring intently at the design process as the means whereby we start to build sustainable communities.

PRINCIPLE

11

Place faith in the design process and engage with it. Understand that drawing is an essential tool of design, not for presenting finished ideas but for exploring them and improving them. A drawing is just a mark on some paper, it's just an idea.

Design According to NASA

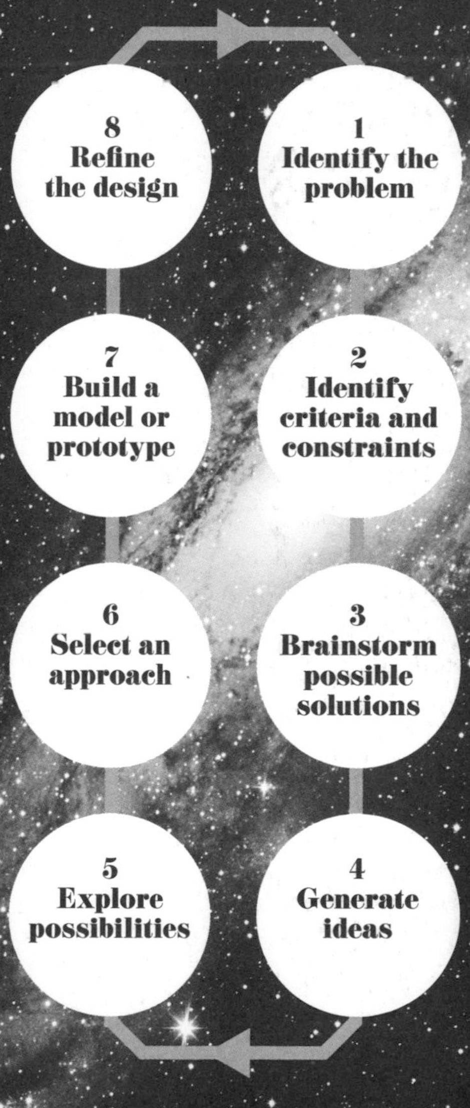

1
Identify the problem
2
Identify criteria and constraints
3
Brainstorm possible solutions
4
Generate ideas
5
Explore possibilities
6
Select an approach
7
Build a model or prototype
8
Refine the design

PRINCIPLE
12

**Regular maintenance
is the most practical
and economic form of
preservation.***

*Society for the Protection
 of Ancient Buildings
 (SPAB) principle

13

NARRATIVE

As good buildings age, the bond with their sites strengthens. A beautiful, interesting or simply ancient building still belongs where it stands, however corrupted that place may have become. Use and adaptation of buildings leave their marks and these, in time, we also see as aspects of the building's integrity.*

*SPAB principle

Leave a building alone and it will form a meaningful relationship with where it is. The sun will bleach bits of it; moss and algae will populate it according to wind direction and orientation. People will wear it as they use it and as those uses change over the decades. Nature will eventually grow into it and it will crumble into nature. But all these things are part of a building's 'settling in' to where it is. They give the place what some people call 'character' but I prefer to call it 'narrative': a story. The power of narrative in buildings and in the built environment is monumental. It's what helps us to make sense of history, and history helps us to make sense of the present.

As part of that narrative, just as buildings are made using hundreds of different processes, dozens of materials and tens of thousands of components, so everyday use and wear of door handles, doors, floorboards, skirting board, dado rails and kitchen sink leave their mark. When people fall in love with old

places, very often they're falling in love with that wear and use, because it represents the imagined lives of others, the sense of historical usage of a building. Living in an old place makes it easier to imagine yourself in the 18th century, for example.

What gives old buildings their charm is not, I believe, any psychic aura or ghostly spirituality. I don't believe buildings resonate to what's gone on in them as though, like a cello, the body of a building vibrates to the echo of the lives of the people that lived there. That's rubbish.

But if the character, the 'beauty and romance', are bound up in the wear and tear of a place, then why do so many owners of old houses tear into them and install their own new incarnations of the place? I've never understood why you would want to rip a place apart in the name of making it 'comfortable'. If you want under-floor heating, buy a new place. Because if you destroy the delicate story of a building in the process of 'modernizing' it, you might as well have bought a new place.

LEFT: Sker House, a Grade 1 listed building on the Glamorgan coast in Wales, was abandoned by its owners in 1977. Restoration work by the Buildings at Risk Trust took place between 1999 and 2003.

99

BUILDINGS

PRINCIPLE
14

Respect the character of old buildings and cherish their idiosyncrasies and imperfections. The character of a place consists of a thousand tiny details which can carelessly be 'improved' into mediocrity.

15

DESIGN EXCELLENCE

Make the context of where you live part of the narrative of your home. Research local history, start a local food network, memorize your landmarks and visit the places of interest and history on your doorstep. Study the flora, fauna and geology of your place, even if it is intensely urban. Invent a story for your place.

Engineers, marketing consultants, biochemists all use the design process. It is time honoured. Design incorporates philosophical discussion and scientific enquiry. Design includes time for research and reflection and the reabsorption of new data and ideas. Design can also embody the spirit of an age and cultural values. At its best it can improve the world and it can make things robust, easy to use and a pleasure, be that a building, a city or a spoon. It can provide those timeless values of Firmness, Commodity and Delight. And, I would add, a standard of excellence that no other process can match.

Design can also not only respond to context but has the magical ability to create context, by making objects, buildings and places that are really good of their sort. It can invent narrative and character and interest. Which, we might all subjectively agree, are good things because they make you feel better. With a little money and when imagination and time and human energy are in relative abundance, design can do this extremely well. Which means it has the ability to make a contribution to the sense of a place, which in turn can enrich our experience of being in a place and lead us to spend time there and respect it. These are fundamental requirements of good 'social sustainability'.

One final idea exercises me and it's something I will explore in the last part of this book. I've always instinctively felt and publicly maintained that good design – be it an AppleMac laptop, a great spoon or a great building – makes you feel better. It can make you feel like a better human being. But can a building go further? Can it make you a better citizen? Can it make you healthier? Or happier?

PRINCIPLE
16

Demand high-quality design in your home and high-quality work. You deserve it and so does the building.

PRINCIPLE

17

New work should express modern needs in a modern language. These are the only terms in which new can relate to old in a way that is positive and responsive at the same time. If an addition proves essential, it should not be made to out-do or out-last the original.*

*SPAB principle

PRINCIPLE

18

Design makes existence better so that we don't have to struggle through it. Use it.

Chapter Eight

LOOKING AFTER THE ELDERLY

Place is a funny thing. It is more than where we live or work and more than a fixed point on the planet. Place can help us make sense of who we are. Providing we can divine the clues that make it up. Most people who have spent a lifetime somewhere are content to define their connection with a place in simple terms. 'I couldn't live anywhere else. My family are from here'. And one's connection to a place can grow remarkably quickly.

I speak from experience. My family are from Scotland and Northern Ireland, sailors for several centuries who migrated to the north of England. There's some European blood there too. My parents were born in the land of Yorkshire, where I was christened. But I grew up in the ambiguous countryside north of London. For over 20 years I've lived in Somerset, surrounded coincidentally by three aunts who independently moved to the balmy and beautiful West Country from the bleak mudflats and wolds of south-east Yorkshire. My mother lives abroad and one brother has taken Australian nationality, now that he is raising a family there; he joins cousins whose father moved to Oz in the 1960s. Come to that my own parents had their transit papers and visas ready to make the antipodean move in 1958, when my mother discovered she was pregnant with me. I changed their plans.

So you'll understand that I have difficulty saying where I'm from. Even now I travel all over Britain and Europe to film and work. I like to spend a lot of time in Chamonix in the mountains. But I regard Somerset as my adopted home. I am happy standing on the soil in that part of the world, or more particularly in an area bounded by the towns of Frome, Bruton, Wells and Radstock. I have no ancestral connection to this area, but maybe 20 years is long enough to make a bond with a place.

The geology here is complex. Carboniferous limestone ridges are interspersed with red Devonian sandstone hills and pockets of oolitic stone, clay and fullers' earth rock. I even have an extinct basalt volcano in the neighbouring village. To the east is the great chalk plain of Salisbury; 15 miles to the north are the Cotswold Hills and to the south-west the low marshes of the Somerset Levels. The richness of the stones here means that as you drive across the county, traditional buildings change in their design and materials every half an hour. Flora and trees change too, as does the very shape of the land, from rocky cliffs and gorges to rollicking humps to rolling downland.

You can see it in traditional buildings, of course: in how a roof pitch reflects the use of straw thatch 500 years ago or how the lime pointing in a wall is tinted with a local sand. You can also see it in local culture, in songs, dances, slang and traditions (all of which exist in abundance in Somerset – you only have to scratch the surface). It's there in the landscape too and in new activities like quarrying or industry. I spent several years filming an urban regeneration series in a northern town, Castleford, that was once home to 13 coal pits that now have gone. What I found sad and shocking was how the coal industry and government expunged all traces of the coal workings following their closure to the extent that the town now has a stunted cultural identity: all meaning and camaraderie that existed in the context of that great and dangerous pursuit of mining have been severed and the town has bravely struggled to find a new identity.

CONTEXT

The strongest visual links with place, the strongest contextual ties, are expressed in the way humans claim territory and populate a place. The mountain may be big but it's not as important as the enclosed 30-acre field and whitewashed homestead nearby. A river can be a fabulous visual asset to a place but it only functions as a context when it is used, boated on and crossed. Just as architecture is of, by and for the people, so context is provided by the people in what they do in a place. Otherwise it's just nature.

So old buildings and places are replete with context, because they illustrate a human occupation that has endured. Thank goodness my culture is more evolutionary than revolutionary. We like old houses, or new houses that look old. We dedicate entire rallies to old cars or steam engines. Every year I go to the Bath and West Fair where enthusiasts demonstrate model traction engines driving model hay balers with model belts, producing model hay bales, each the size of a Tetra Pak carton.

PRINCIPLE
19

The strongest visual links with place, the strongest contextual ties, are expressed in the way humans claim territory and populate a place. The mountain may be big but it's not as important as the enclosed 30-acre field and whitewashed homestead nearby. A river can be a fabulous visual asset to a place but it functions as a context only when it is used, boated on and crossed. Just as architecture is of, by and for the people, so context is provided by the people in what they do in a place. Otherwise it's just nature.

RIGHT: A thatched cottage in the Chilterns

CONSERVATION

Even our historical societies themselves are old. Soon there'll be a Society for the Preservation of Historical Societies. Or there would be if these groups weren't so alive and thriving. The Society for the Protection of Ancient Buildings (of which I have been a member for some 30 years) is itself ancient, having been founded by William Morris in anger in 1877 on seeing the damage being wrought to the fabric of our churches and cathedrals in the name of well-meaning 'restoration',

a by-word for complete replacement and renewal. It's the paramilitary wing of the heritage movement, also known as the 'Leave it Alone Society'.

The society's roles are laudable: to promote 'conservative repair' wherever possible, not restoration; to encourage repair work that is delicate and obvious and not fake history; to train and educate craftsmen; and to stimulate research and casework on old buildings that collectively enhance our

understanding of the context and archaeology of our historic environment. Authenticity is a big word for the SPAB and so is Romance: this is an organization in love with every crumb of every old building, just as steam enthusiasts are with every spline of every cog of every miniature baler.

It is also a body before which all applications to demolish or partly demolish

BELOW: The mid-fifteenth-century Peel Castle, near Skipton, Yorkshire, before its restoration (left) and after (right)

listed buildings are passed, so it is difficult to overplay the importance of the SPAB in helping define how our built environment should be looked after. English Heritage is a pup by comparison and its approaches have always been influenced and informed by its wiser, elder sibling. I'm grateful for the intellectual scaffolding that the SPAB has constructed over the past 134 years which has helped me repair two listed houses. But that scaffolding and the edifice within it, built of casework and

documentary research that now spans three centuries, is under threat. Inevitably, an evolutionary institution like the SPAB changes slowly and cautiously. The illustrated *Old House Handbook* by Marianne Suhr and Roger Hunt, published recently, is a brilliant, accessible and modest updating of Morris's philosophy. At the same time, English Heritage has produced an impressive 70-page document, Conservation Principles, which rewrites our entire approach to how we

view, manage and adapt our historic environment, from streets to tumuli to country mansions to coastline.

Conservation Principles reflects the character of English Heritage's boss, Dr Simon Thurley. It's a handsome document, thoughtfully composed with scholarly rigour and intellectual grist. It's almost got a floppy blonde fringe. You can see the Spabians, blinking on the shores of Spabia, as they examine the impending tsunami of change in their

world, their tweed armour first ruffled by the terror of change, only to be smoothed by the zephyr breeze of Thurley's voice.

The new big Principles sweepingly acknowledge and accommodate the SPAB's view of the world. But they also subtly mark out a new direction for how we manage the fabric of history, suggesting occasional 'restoration' or even dramatic reconstruction of buildings and places. English Heritage wants to provide a positive and pragmatic framework for developers. It even suggests that commercial considerations should drive how we treat old buildings.

I've seen the effects of this new attitude nowhere more noticeably than in the restoration of Peel Castle (shown on the previous pages) in Yorkshire, a project we filmed over three years for my television series *Grand Designs*. In the theocratic state of Spabia, the owners, Francis and Karen Shaw, might have been allowed to gently

repair the walls of the old castle and live perhaps in one half, in some kind of modern addition floating within the ancient structure. Spabian law dictates that every component and problem in a building is treated on its own merit within the overall context of the building. Solutions are often hyper-localized, which means that it is impossible to draw generalities. This makes for a huge body of casework upon which the SPAB can draw. The work reflects the cool scientific approaches of enquiry, research and empiricism; the society's principles and philosophy provide a reference framework.

In the hyper-accessible and liberal land of Thurleya, the owners, Karen and Francis Shaw, were allowed to follow a much more pragmatic and inventive route, converting (for the first time ever, it would seem) a Scheduled Ancient Monument for habitation, delicately repairing some areas (entirely at one with SPAB principles) whilst elsewhere devising programmes for

restoration, speculative theatrical reconstruction and original new build. This flouted SPAB principles because it confusingly mixed old and new and employed pastiche – or 'loving homage', if you like – in an approach that was unthinkable 10 years ago; it is still highly controversial within the corridors and winding staircases of the SPAB and it was only made possible in Yorkshire thanks to the ministry of Karen's and Francis's EH officer, Keith Emerick, who directed the philosophy of the project and himself had a role in determining the contents of the new Conservation Principles.

We were enormously lucky in being able, over those three years, to chart the evolution of change within English Heritage and film an outcome that was enormously positive, and has saved a building. If that is what the new Conservation Principles are designed to deliver, then bring 'em on. But I'm not going to relinquish my SPAB membership.

PRINCIPLE

20

Conservation is the process of managing change to a significant place in its setting in ways that will best sustain its heritage values, while recognizing opportunities to reveal or reinforce those values for present and future generations.*

*English Heritage conservation principle

PATRIMONIO

Meanwhile, further afield, other countries are moving faster than the UK. The French, for example, take building conservation seriously but are more concerned with the overall aesthetic impact of what they do. If the Brits like narrative, the French like pictures. Somewhat like the Italians, who dote on the idea of landscape and setting as much as they do on buildings. They even have a word for it, which eludes speakers of the English language: patrimonio. It finds equal popularity in France as patrimoine but doesn't stand for much in English as 'patrimony', which most people would consider as belonging to the language of lawyers. Our nearest equivalent examples of it are National Parks and Conservation Areas. One deals with landscape, the other with collections of buildings in conurbations. 'Patrimony' expresses an idea that is bigger than the both of them together: an idea of connection to a place, its distinctive identity and an authenticity that emerges from the relationship between what has been, what is there and how we perceive it now.

The obvious example I can think of is Tuscany. This Italian region, also known as Chiantishire on account of the number of Brits living there, is as appealing and delightful as any in the world – because of its patrimonio. I've worked on the repair and restoration of buildings in Tuscany where sometimes not a moment is spent debating whether to mend buildings with sympathetic materials. To the south of the region, which is an earthquake zone (you may remember the devastating quake in Aquila and that which destroyed much of Giotto's work in the chapel at Assisi), there is a prerequisite to fill the foundations of every old building with reinforced concrete, repair the walls with cement and hidden seismic bricks, and then finally point the stonework with traditional lime mortar to give an authentic impression. This inevitably leads to a more superficial and aesthetic treatment of buildings and locality, the results of which are very tidy, over-restored villages. Come to that, entire swathes of landscape seem to have been repointed to a hypothetical historical

Villa Il Belvedere in Tuscany, Italy, encircled by cypresses

state, a sort of mish-mash of painting backgrounds from the Renaissance to the Ottocento. Merchant Ivory meets Masaccio.

The result is charming, a filmic experience that stimulates your own fuzzy memory of once having seen a landscape painting with some dogs running through umbrella pines by a very famous 15th-century painter whose name temporarily escapes you. Or is it that film with Helena Bonham-Thingy as a wild Edwardian English girl who loses her spiritual virginity to the pantheistic cypress groves? You know, the one based on the book by whatsisname?

Patrimonio is big context and, unlike the rough tweeds of a bespectacled man from the SPAB, can be soft and unchallenging and sometimes not difficult to achieve if you're prepared to ride roughshod over a lot of particular, small and inconvenient detail in a place. The change in render or pointing detail from one home to another, the 1920s extension, the window or

shutter that might be a 20th-century copy or might just be the last remnant from a lost, earlier tradition: they risk being lost. And there lies the rub. Conservation produces buildings of immense character and quirky idiosyncrasy full of historical detail. Patrimony provides the immense gesture, the great sweep, which, frankly, is more enjoyable.

America has taken the idea of patrimony to its obvious paradigm. The historical villages of Colonial Williamsburg and Shaker villages such as Pleasant Hill and Canterbury are living museums which are but a stone's throw from what Walt Disney produced in his 'Main Streets' and Wild West frontier towns of

his theme-park franchise. These are as brilliantly done with authentic materials, much craftsmanship and as much fakery as goes into the average living museum. The evolution of this idea is Seaside, Walt's ideal village, built in historical style according to New Urbanist principles and full of patrimonious references to the traditional building types of early America. It is beguiling because it tugs at the heart, not the mind, and in the matters of home, heart wins. Seaside appeals hugely and houses there sell at a significant premium. Britain does 'old' as scratchy nerdism; Europe does it as a pragmatically organized tourist attraction; America sells you the dream.

66 Patrimony expresses an idea of connection to a place, its distinctive identity and an authenticity that emerges from the relationship between what has been, what is there and how we perceive it now. 99

RIGHT: Villa Cimbrone, Ravello, Italy

SEASIDE FLORIDA
REAL ESTATE
Shingle Villa, Sail Loft Boulevard

" The city of Seaside made a giant splash in the architectural world when developer Robert Davis carved out a modern Victorian town with narrow streets, picket fences and homes arranged close together to encourage walking and neighbourliness. It was the first of its kind, creating the model for towns across America. Seaside's 'walk-to-anywhere' design is working to bring necessary shops and services to its residents and guests, including a post office and a school. Seaside, Florida's centrepiece, contains the market, art galleries, a florist, an ice cream store, a post office, and other small boutiques. Although many Seaside Florida rental homes can be rented on a daily or weekly basis, the city of Seaside also offers a motor court and bed and breakfast. Park your car and rent bicycles to explore this wildly successful pioneering town, featured in the 1997 motion picture *The Truman Show*. You still have the opportunity to purchase Seaside Florida Real Estate. "

PRINCIPLE
21

Demand interest and originality in your public realm. Look for clues to its identity and celebrate the local uniqueness of where you live.

Chapter Nine

COMFORT AND JOY

I should really have called this tiny chapter the 'Joy of Comfort', because it deals with the very pragmatic but essential way in which we try to get the physical world to mould itself to us. I don't mean the way we like what we build to psychologically mould itself to our identities, but how a door handle should fit any one of 5,000 different hands and still feel comfortable and enjoyable to use for all of the hands' owners.

I once designed a range of bathroom fittings that were intended as the antidote for all those masculine, overtly engineered towel rails that look as though somebody has raided the parts bin at Boeing. I was interested in the fluid forms that metal takes on when it melts and wanted shapes that fitted the hands as comfortably as good cutlery does, or a German car-door handle. For a while I contemplated making prototypes in Plasticine and even tried squeezing some in my fists to see the shapes that would emerge. They were good and fluid looking but the trouble was they fitted my hands and not those of my friends or children.

There is no universally valid, ergonomic design that will suit everybody, because we are such wildly different shapes. The Eames recliner is ridiculously small for me at 6 feet 2 inches. The first time I tried sitting in this icon of the 20th century it was a crashing disappointment that left me wondering if I had been born into the wrong age. Finding comfort – the joy of a comfortable chair or door handle – is to be prized above fashion, style, image – or cool design, which is just another term for fashion, style and image. Comfort is the most civilizing aspect of design or architecture. Seek it out.

PRINCIPLE
22

Any man-made thing should be well made and durable; it should be ergonomic and fit for purpose; it should have brought no harm to anybody or anything; and it should evoke delight and lasting pleasure in use.

PRINCIPLE
23

Finding comfort – the joy of a comfortable chair or door handle – is to be prized above fashion, style and image. Comfort is the most civilizing aspect of design or architecture. Seek it out.

NOISE

People have different levels of resistance to noise, and this is not related to how deaf they are. Hardly surprising when you consider that the ear can hear extremely quiet sounds from that of breathing at about 10 decibels (dB) up to sounds with an energy level 10 billion times greater – the maximum allowed at a rock concert. A rise of 10 dB in sound level corresponds roughly to a doubling of subjective loudness. Therefore a sound of 80 dB is twice as loud as a sound of 70 dB which is twice as loud as a sound of 60 dB. Correspondingly, the 80 dB sound is four times louder than the 60 dB sound.

So you need to be prepared to accept that what is a tolerable level of noise for you may not be so for someone you live or work with. The first rule in combating noise is to reduce its power at source – turn the music volume down, ask someone to be quieter – although your chances of achieving what you want in your

> **❝ Noise complaints are the most common complaints made to housing authorities and governments. ❞**

neighbourhood are small: noise complaints are the most common complaints made to housing authorities and governments. The second line of defence is to insulate yourself: close the door or window; use a variety of insulating materials in the construction of your home (different materials will counteract different frequency ranges); board your room out with sound-absorbing sheets underneath the plasterboard; use acoustic boards for your ceiling; buy rubber mats to mount your kitchen appliances on. The third line of defence is to fight noise with noise: wear headphones and listen to music; install a fountain in your garden as an aural focal point to drown out the sound of traffic and aircraft.

KITCHEN CULTURE

The designer Johnny Grey has spent a working life figuring out how the kitchen should best be laid out. In his book, Kitchen Culture, he summarizes in a few pages the distilled common sense that's required when laying out any hard-working room. The key points are few but illuminating. I've included a picture from his volume as illustration.

Sink Height

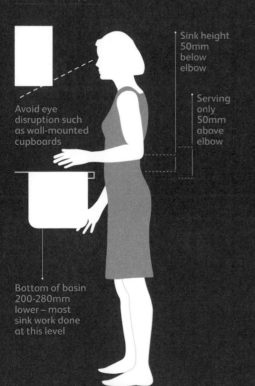

Avoid eye disruption such as wall-mounted cupboards

Sink height 50mm below elbow

Serving only 50mm above elbow

Bottom of basin 200-280mm lower – most sink work done at this level

1. Each task demands a set of mindful body mechanics and good design to help provide maximum comfort and avoidance of injury.

2. When accessing a low cupboard, movement should come from the knee joint. Keep the spine straight and bend from the hips, not the neck.

3. The key measurement should be taken from the client's flexed elbow height (FE). Food preparation needs to be done on a surface 75mm below FE height. Washing up needs to be done on a surface 50mm below FE height (because the bottom of the bowl is much lower). Cooking needs to be lower to avoid fat splashing, at around 75–100mm below FE.

4. The oven door should be no higher than waist height.

5. Key storage areas should be at 1–1.25 metres from the floor.

6. Worktops should be 600–750mm deep. Expect a maximum reach of 1.8 metres across this without moving your legs.

7. Avoid long distances between work areas but allow ample space to circulate around an open oven or other machine.

8. Employ 'soft' geometry: rounded corners and edges, and forms which fit the fluidity of circulation.

TEMPERATURE

As with noise, we have different comfort levels when it comes to ambient temperature, but humans have certain thresholds which it is dangerous to exceed. Prolonged exposure at freezing temperatures will cut off circulation, and body temperatures above the norm of 37°C will invoke abnormal brain activity – just as fevers do. To manage body temperature, humans employ a number of mechanisms, some of them automatic like shivering and sweating and some of them conscious such as exercise and choosing lighter or warmer clothes. The environmental engineer Max Fordham has a number of observations about these processes, chief among which is that people do not enjoy constancy and relish the opportunity to react to changes in the environment, breezes and changes in temperature. We are biologically programmed to enjoy this reaction and become bored if our home and working environment is kept static.

'Just as we enjoy making physical movements as exercise for our muscles, so we can also experience pleasure by making adjustments for body temperature . . . The current engineering consensus, which has been reached by asking people whether they are 'too hot' or 'too cold', has arrived at a very narrow definition of a comfortable temperature. It does not allow for people making their own adjustments as small variations of temperature occur. This not only means that we use more carbon fuel, but also seems to lead to complaints by the occupants of the building, who feel they have no control.'

This view concurs with the designers of the UK Department of the Environment building in Bristol (below), who furnished the block with openable windows. The project architect I spoke to there was astonished to discover that having a minimum of control over their environment seemed to lead employees to feel better and take off fewer days sick. As Max Fordham puts it: 'Research shows that people are more comfortable, and happy, when they can make adjustments in response to varying conditions. We can adjust the heat loss from the skin by covering a chosen area of it with clothes. We can adjust the thickness and insulation value of the clothes.'

In an age of shell suits and T-shirts we have forgotten this art of adjustment.

GET YOUR CIRCULATION GOING

It is a little known truth that the most comfortable homes are those in which it is easy to move around. Max Beerbohm described the greatest English sport as that of 'furniture dodging' as we, as one nation, negotiate the curse of the brown furniture inherited from a maiden aunt. I've never been so unlucky as to inherit furniture, as my family's sport was to chop it up for firewood. Instead I've always taken to drawing out the 'circulation' of people in a building whenever planning a home (see my drawing). I use fat arrows and lines for principal routes, which will in turn demand wider spaces to move through as more people try to pass, carrying homework, shopping, dog in disgrace, etc. For smaller routes I use narrower arrows and the result is a layout that always works.

Chapter Ten

ARCHI-TECTURE AFTER DARK

It's impossible to talk about buildings and the built world without talking about light. Sure, we can touch objects and buildings, and tactility provides an important way of understanding our world. But there is a difference in scale and comprehension between a spoon and a cathedral. You could never, without sight, understand St Paul's Cathedral by touch alone, nor ever understand its context in the City of London.

Sight, for those of us lucky enough to be blessed with it, provides comprehension. The 17th-century clergyman Thomas Fuller described how 'Light, God's eldest daughter, is a principal beauty in a building.' And so it is. Without light, there is no vision and little sense. Without light there would have been no need to build St Paul's with a dome or portico. Or windows. It could have been made as a large, plain box. G.K. Chesterton wrote that all architecture is great architecture after sunset. He should have said that no architecture is great architecture after sunset.

If you have ever stood in or outside a sunlit classical building and seen a shaft of light fall across a cornice, or ever admired the texture of bricks, or ever seen the glimmer of a reflected sun in the glass wall of a skycraper, you will know what I mean. Regardless of materials and style, light doesn't just help us understand architecture: it brings it to life, and it helps us love it.

There are two ways in which daylight does this. First, it defines the mouldings, the forms and the details of a structure and it does this by creating shadow. Without shadow, everything would appear flat. One of the biggest challenges confronting north European architects in the 20th century was how to make flat-walled Modernism look as striking and interesting in grey cloudy light as it did in the baking sunshine of Le Corbusier's Marseille. Shadow is architecture's friend and in a way more important than light, because it is the shadows that we read, not the highlights. Shadow exists as a multiplicity of tones.

Second, daylight employs movement to make buildings interesting. Clouds move across a sky and are reflected in windows; they reveal sunlight at differing intensities and levels of sharpness as the sun is hidden and then exposed; the wind moves trees and the leaves cast dancing shadows on a wall; the sun circles across the sky, moving around a building, and the shadows lengthen, changing colour as they do; the sun itself changes colour and tints the buildings; as we enter, our eyes adjust and the shadows move to become subtly lit in the change of exposure.

The evolution of architectural styles, from that of the Ionic Greek temple, through Palladio, Gothic tracery and Modernism, depended on and responded to the light from the sun. Le Corbusier, the 20th-century founder of Modernism, described architecture as a 'learned game, correct and magnificent, of forms assembled in light' and wrote that 'Our eyes are constructed to enable us to see forms in light.'

Getting architecture to work under artificial lighting is painfully difficult. The eye is a demanding organ, searching to understand sense and order on the one hand whilst greedy for complexity and subtlety on the other. So how do you design your lighting at home? After the sun has gone down, that is.

LIGHTING

Once upon a time people burnt oil in a lamp to see by. Now we burn oil in power stations and consider ourselves very clever for doing so. The electric lamp has given us a welter of different lighting sources (fluorescent, tungsten, halogen and so on) and some very odd-shaped bulbs too, which we can shade, direct, reflect, soften, sharpen and dim in the way we never could an oil lamp or candle.

Task lighting

Task lighting is perhaps the dullest area for your average lighting designer but it is fundamental to human beings. It should light not us, or even the building in particular, but what we do in a building. Task lighting illuminates a corridor to walk down, a picture to look at; it lights work surfaces, the patch of eiderdown where we prop our book in bed, the homework table and the lap on the sofa when we want to read a paper or darn a sock. It should never, by contrast, point at the eye. It is the most important type of lighting.

Ambient lighting

Ambient lighting is that soft, droolly background lighting you get in expensive hotels and bars. It's mood lighting and you can't really see where it's coming from. Come to that you can't really see your watch to tell what time it is under a scheme that uses nothing but ambient lighting. The best ambient schemes uplight ceilings as giant reflectors providing the artificial equivalent to a cloudy day: all-over background light with no real shadows. Very easy on the eye and the complement to task lighting. Table lamps with big shades dotted around a room will uplight the ceiling, providing soft ambient light as well as some directed downlight for tasks.

Directional lighting

Directional lighting is beloved of interior designers because it illuminates their work. It's task lighting but pointing the other way, at the building: the spot illuminating the alcove or the row of downlighters pointing at the swirly rug. Nearly every amateur lighting designer makes the mistake of thinking this is the most important kind of lighting to put in their home. It isn't. It's the least important.

Decorative lighting

Decorative lighting is the fun stuff, the chandelier that says 'look at me', the heartwarming candelabra or colour-changing inflatable Christmas tree. Decorative light is glamour and twinkle and that's it.

Kinetic lighting

Kinetic lighting is the most atavistic and psychologically powerful of all kinds of light. It is the movement of the sun and the dancing shadows of trees, the dancing candle flame that brings shadows alive and the open fire. This primitive potency explains the attraction of naff flame-effect electric fires and also explains why people are prepared to watch so much drivel on television: the TV is the latter-day hearth; we can read into its dancing blue flames all our imaginings.

IN THE RIGHT ORDER

Start a scheme by appealing to the eye's need for order and sense. Figure out where the task lighting is going – above kitchen work tables, for example. Bathrooms do not need directional lighting but do need high levels of all-round lighting near a mirror (think of theatrical make-up mirrors encircled with bulbs) for face inspection, shaving and make-up. Task lighting around a sofa in the middle of a room may need floor sockets placed near by. Don't rely on downlighters to do all your task lighting and do use opaque shades to avoid glare and to act as reflectors, directing the maximum amount of light to the task. Close work such as model-making or sewing requires many times the amount of light needed for reading or cooking.

PRINCIPLE

24

Gardens need very little lighting. We are a world of nature's children, in love with the stars, and to see them at all requires very low levels of illumination.

The enemy of friendship is the halogen downlighter

Halogen spots were invented to display goods in retail environments, where they were pointed away from customers towards the merchandise. They are bright and direct, casting sharp shadows. So don't fill your house with them unless you plan to open a bakery there. People look awful and haggard under a direct, vertical spotlight. They won't thank you for tricksy lighting.

The enemy of a good lighting scheme is glare

It's tiring and can temporarily blind the eye. Do not expose your lighting sources if you can help it. Halogen downlighters in a ceiling are usually an appalling source of glare because they are placed so close to the surface. You'll notice that in the best public buildings the spotlights are recessed, often in black tubes, and therefore hidden – unless you look directly straight up. Place uplighters above eye level and shade bulbs carefully.

PEOPLE LOOK GOOD IN AMBIENT LIGHT

Ambient light can take 20 years off someone's face, which is why photographers use giant reflectors when shooting someone – especially outside on a sunny day – to 'fill' the features and shadows and obliterate the wrinkles. Indoors, soft general lighting will do the same thing. It also makes for a very relaxing state and is the only kind of lighting you should have in a room if all you do is work on a screen – although a balanced level of task lighting is also usually needed on a table. Watching television is best done in ambient light.

LEDs

Light-emitting diodes are super efficient, meaning that for just a few meagre watts, a downlighter or bulb will produce the same output as a conventional lamp many times its wattage. A 60-watt halogen spot can be imitated with a much bulkier compact fluorescent of about 11 watts and a tiny 6- or 7-watt LED. I could not have written that sentence a year ago and I dare say a year from now there will be LED lamps in stores that double that performance. A major impediment with LEDs is that for decades they could be made in red, blue, green and amber but never white. Until somebody had the brilliant idea of wrapping the same glowing white phosphor coating that is used in fluorescent tubes around the LED and tweaking the blue light to stimulate those phosphors. Result: a white LED. With all the attractive, ghoulish tints traditionally associated with fluorescent lighting. A white LED, it turns out, is just a very, very compact fluorescent. The good news is that LEDs are finally now available in both warm and cool white. Cool white presumably for submarine use.

KELVIN IS NOT MY NAME

The common perception is that fluorescent lights produce an other-worldly glow that would seem appropriate on a submarine or alien spacecraft, rendering objects cold and people positively ghoulish. To be fair, fluorescent tubes have advanced in performance in leaps and bounds. I now use 'warm' tubes hidden behind a suspended platform in my kitchen to produce a really pleasant creamy glow. You wouldn't know they were fluoros.

How we perceive the 'colour' and the 'temperature' of lighting depends partly on the colour rendering of the light source (and the degree of balance with which it illuminates the full colour spectrum) but for practical everyday use it depends mainly on the colour temperature of the light source (its yellowness, blueness or whiteness), which you can check on the packet if you know what to look for – just as you might look for hydrogenated vegetable oil on a packet of biscuits. A colour temperature of 3,500K (for Kelvin, the man who invented this arcane form of referencing) or above will probably be too white or bluish for your tastes. 3,000K is around the colour of a typical halogen downlighter, 2,700K corresponds to a nice warm tungsten light and, if you're intent on reproducing historical lighting settings, 1,500K is the orange colour of a candle. Not that you'll find a fluorescent light in that colour. Best, if you're not technically minded, to look for bulbs that are labelled 'warm white' and in my view you can't do much worse than buy Philips Softone or Megaman warm white compact fluorescent lamps ('lamp', while we're being specific, being the trade term for 'bulb') and Osram Dulux warm fluorescent tubes.

PLAY AT BEING YOUR OWN LIGHTING DESIGNER

Before you commit to designing a room or a house, take a large, reflective aluminium saucepan or a wok lid and a car inspection lamp on a long extension lead. Play at directing the light from the lamp with the wok lid. This is an unrivalled way of designing your own lighting scheme. Outdoors you don't even need a saucepan and a lightbulb. In my infant days as a lighting designer I put clever uplighters and reflectors in my garden but then later ripped them all out. Now, I just use some solar-powered downlighters to show me where the path is and a few candles now and then. My friend, the lighting designer Bruce Munro, showed me his trick for lighting a path on a party night: put candles or night lights inside old jam jars inside white paper bags.

PRINCIPLE

25

There are five important types of lighting to use in a home. Task lighting, the most important, should light not us, or even the building in particular, but what we do in a building. Ambient lighting provides the artificial equivalent to a cloudy day: all-over background light with no real shadows. Directional lighting is the least important. It is the spotlamp illuminating the alcove or the row of downlighters pointing at the swirly rug. Decorative lighting is glamour and twinkle and that's it. Kinetic lighting is the most atavistic and psychologically powerful of all. It is the movement of the sun and the dancing shadows of trees, the dancing candle flame that brings shadows alive and the open fire.

PART THREE

THIN

Chapter Eleven

HOW TO SHOP

You wouldn't think anybody needed to be told how to shop, would you? It's something we're all used to doing and have been ever since a grunty man in a furry leotard tried to exchange a dead pig for a bag of sticks. That particular transaction was based on need, and reciprocal need at that. 'I need those sticks; you're going to need this pig at the weekend; grunt, let's swap.'

Millions of other transactions followed in which reciprocity, which was not always shared, gave way to an exchangeable token that could be used later when real need did arise.

The problem with money is not that tokens and IOUs are a bad idea. Far from it: in a sophisticated society, money allows us to trade our labour for things we need when we need them, or to save or borrow so that we have tokens to pay for the big expenditures in life – things like fast cars and divorce.

No, the real problem with money is desire. Whereas Gruntman made his purchases entirely according to what he needed, we can go out and spend only to satisfy our desire. We don't trade any more, we shop. What's worse is that Gruntman got his kicks, his dopamine hit, every time he went out to chase another pig while we, despite our ever-so-sophisticated lifestyle, still need that same dopamine hit. And guess what delivers that hit time after time? The purchase. Shoppig. I mean shopping.

There's no such thing as retail therapy, just retail addiction. But in life we are all faced with the need to buy both the basics, like food and clothing, and the extraordinary purchases, like kitchens and holidays. Other than reading consumer magazines and looking at price-comparison websites, what are the guiding principles to good shopping?

BUY ETHICALLY

Sounds a nightmare, doesn't it? How on earth are you supposed to buy a table lamp or a pair of jeans when you can't even buy a bag of tomatoes ethically? But of course you can buy a bag of tomatoes ethically. When you and I are standing in a supermarket, we're subject to all kinds of powerful, manipulating visual merchandising tactics. We should be putty in Wal-Mart's hands, yet we're still able to make some independent decisions ourselves. In fact, it turns out we can operate quite sophisticated scales of value judgement if we choose. To be frank, I try not to find myself in supermarkets, preferring the farm shop or the small retailer. That's the first decision I take. If I'm in Tesco looking for apples, the first question I'll ask is are they local? After which I ask myself if they're organic. Followed by whether they're Fairtrade. And finally whether they are on offer.

I can juggle these values, inserting new ones like 'free-range' or 'home-grown', and I can use my wits to separate out truth from fiction, avoiding the traps set by retailers with words like 'luxury', 'authentic' and 'farm fresh'. If it's farm fresh, what's it doing in a supermarket?

My point is that if we can do this in a supermarket, why can't we operate the same way when buying a sofa or a vase? Well, the real problem here is lack of information. The food lobbies have been busy for decades persuading manufacturers and supermarkets to provide accurate, authenticated information about foodstuffs, with the result that we have come to trust the Fairtrade logo and the Soil Association organic label, for example. Our value systems can depend on solid information. Meanwhile there's nothing on my sofa to tell me whether it was made in Milan or Manila. I learned only recently that all the sofas sold in Britain by Marks & Spencer are made not in the Far East but in a small factory in Wales.

It's easier when you come to buy building materials: basic stuffs like cement, lime and aggregate have

to be certified; and timber – and furniture for both the home and the garden – can be bought with the Forest Stewardship Council (FSC) logo. It is possible, if you look hard enough and ask hard enough, to divine the source and the environmental and human impact of most things that we buy.

But it still seems that we prefer not to ask. In 2006 I was sufficiently inspired by the idea of ethical home shopping to be persuaded to help set up an ethical mail-order company selling furniture, fabrics and accessories. We worked with British-based designers, created a crafts-based culture, used small, family-based factories, used only FSC timbers and were in the process of Fairtrade accreditation. At that time footballs, bizarrely, were the only non-food item to carry a Fairtrade logo; our products never did because the business punctured, went phutt and got kicked into the stand, never to be seen again. There were lots of reasons why it went under but one painful explanation was that the market was just not ready, just didn't care enough, to want to have to think about 'how ethical' a chair or a place mat might be. I am ever hopeful. Indeed I lobby for more transparent retail. But it is sometimes difficult when I'm repeatedly told that Britain, my home country, is still the largest importer of illegal timber in Europe.

Demand to know where things come from, what is in them, who has made them and under what conditions. Do not be led only by price but look for value and craftsmanship. Buy only things and materials that respect the human energy that has gone into them and where the maker is rewarded fairly.

Buy branded

By which I mean reputable. I also mean do not buy branded at almost any cost. Brand used to stand for a company with a good name, a factory not far from where you lived and a proud reputation. A brand nowadays usually represents a company that used to have a good name but which has diversified way beyond its core activities, doesn't have any factories any more and buys crap from the Far East with its name on it.

Recontextualize

Buy recontextualized stuff – in other words objects that are revitalized through being remade. In my local town is a seamstress with a shop selling clothes entirely made from other clothes. There's a furniture maker who reassembles five old broken chests of drawers into one new one. This is what you'd call creative recycling, not just finding new uses for raw materials but new incarnations for finished objects, or bits of them at least.

For that matter, buy secondhand

Other people's stuff already has a story – though not one that you'll always want to remember. It all depends how many hands an object has passed through: the more hands, the more the piece qualifies as an antique and is desirable for its 'patina' and signs of wear and tear; the fewer hands, the more it feels like a cast-off. My solution is to mix up the brand-new, the inherited, the cast-offs and the antiques. That way, my home doesn't feel full of other people's stuff, but my own.

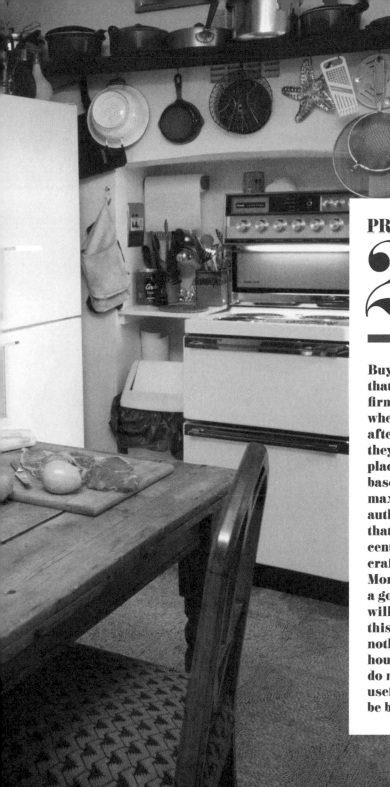

PRINCIPLE
27

Buy authentic. Stuff that is made in a firm's own factories where they look after the people they employ and the place where they're based. A crucial maxim of buying authentically is that of the 19th-century writer and craftsman William Morris: 'If you want a golden rule that will fit everything, this is it: Have nothing in your houses that you do not know to be useful or believe to be beautiful.'

Chapter Twelve
HOW NOT TO SHOP

It's important, amidst hardship and penury, to find pleasure in the non-material, in the 'doing' rather than 'acquiring'. Aristotle would have exhorted us to find the pleasure inherent in our great biological capacity as human beings. John Stuart Mill would have told us to read, think and pursue the higher abstract pleasures. St Augustine would have asked us to look into a flower. I could at this point ramble on about the value of life-long learning and the improving effect of jigsaws or growing your own vegetables, all of which of course are highly pleasurable.

The social psychologist Mihaly Csikszentmihalyi would have endorsed the Aristotelean view of pleasure deriving from doing and told us about his 'flow' theory of being absorbed in an activity. I don't think any of them suggested we should go shopping to make ourselves happy.

For happiness, 'doing' apparently beats 'owning' any day. But I always thought that shopping was in fact quite a sophisticated form of doing. Indeed, Guy McKhann, professor of neurology at Johns Hopkins University, together with his wife, researcher Marilyn Albert, spent ten years studying the productivity of 3,000 elderly people and concluded that shopping combines three elements that help the brain to function better:

1. It involves quite a lot of strenuous effort and keeps people active.

2. It challenges the brain in the way Sudoku and crosswords do, by forcing decisions, forcing abstract thought processes such as imagining how a table lamp will look at home and forcing mental exercises such as the analysis of cost comparisons in, say, three-for-two offers.

3. It gives people a positive self-image: 'They really feel good about themselves, like they've accomplished something,' says McKhann.

It's not difficult for any of us, as shoppers, to recognize these pluses. Who wouldn't, in the easy relaxedness of retirement, derive pleasure from strolling down the high street on a sunny Monday morning to buy the week's vegetables, bumping into friends along the way, enjoying the sociability of the process? Sadly, however, most retail activity takes place in more intense circumstances: on a Saturday in a mall crammed with tens of thousands of people and with your screaming child; in the chaotic pandemonium of a sale; in the chiller aisle of a supermarket at the end of a working day, when you just feel like lying down in the cabinet and allowing yourself to be deep frozen.

And much shopping these days is about acquiring for its own sake. There may be an element of self-fulfilment when the frequent shopper gets out there, but there is a more insidious and addictive side to retail: shopping is an activity that our brain confuses with more primitive activities – those of acquiring territory and knowledge of that territory. When we shop, our

brains get triggered to produce dopamine, a home-brew drug that gives us an instant high of curiosity and anticipation. Whereas, and I give this example for comparison's sake, spending eight months carving a piece of limewood into a miniature Chartres Cathedral produces another mood-improving drug, serotonin, which apparently hangs around longer and induces a calmer and less heightened sense of well-being.

Csikszentmihalyi would have got carving, like St Augustine. In my view, this alternative self-made medication seems more like it and can be found under the bonnet of a car or even in darning a sock. It is the pure satisfaction of craftsmanship.

Yet most of us are easily hooked on dopamine. Any new or exciting experience for a human being, like discovering a herd of antelope ready to be speared and dragged back to the cave for food, or finding a pair of shoes in the right colour, produces the stuff. It hits more effectively when you're on foreign, new territory, as on a shopping trip to New York, or when the discoveries are, on the general scale of things, extraordinary, as during the winter sales or in the furniture department of TK Maxx.

MRI studies of brain activity suggest that surges in dopamine levels are linked much more with the anticipation of an experience than with the experience itself – which may explain why people get so much pleasure out of window shopping or hunting for bargains. Dr Gregory Berns of Emory University says dopamine may help explain why someone buys shoes they never wear. 'You see the shoes and get this burst of dopamine,' which 'motivates you to seal the deal and buy them. It's like a fuel injector for action, but once they're bought it's almost a let down.'

Dopamine can hit high and hard but it drops off quickly, leaving you with a sense of loss or disappointment plus the urge to go out and buy more just to get the rush again. Retail therapy doesn't cure the low; it helps cause it. I think the clue to dopamine might just be in the name.

Since America is the home of shopping, it's not surprising to find that it's also the home of retail psychology, with specialist research departments sprouting at every other university, such as Emory, Kentucky and Indiana. Dr Ruth Engs of the latter august institution has even drawn up a list of shopping do's and don'ts to help compulsive shoe-buyers deal with their dopamine addiction. I think they merit inclusion here because they can very probably help us all to craft our homes to be places that are populated with more craftsmanship and less junk, more autobiographical stuff that means something to us and less show-off bling.

SHOPPING DO'S AND DON'TS

Make a list

Obvious really, but very helpful in avoiding distraction. Buy only the items on your shopping list to avoid impulse purchases.

Don't use credit cards

But use cash or debit cards instead. This creates financial limits and checks your reaction to dopamine production. Don't even think about taking out store credit cards. Leave your wallet at home. This is a form of enforced daylight-hours window shopping that allows you not only to gaze through the glass but also to go into the store, try clothes on and sit on that luxurious sofa, all in total safety.

Don't shop when away

The added novelty of shopping in a new place puts you at higher risk of buying something you don't need because dopamine production is increased when exploring 'new territories'. The very last thing you should be doing is organizing shopping trips to new cities or countries. Try making a model of Chartres Cathedral instead. Or any activity that will produce serotonin.

Window shop...

when the stores are shut after hours. This is an extreme solution but one proven to work. You'll get the pleasure of shopping without the risk of overspending. Or spending even.

Remind yourself...

that, when you get that retail rush, it's just a primitive chemical reaction originally designed to help tribal mankind scope out territory and bag some game for supper. It's deceiving you into thinking you really need that eleventh teapot.

PRINCIPLE 28

You employ the design process when you plan a menu for a dinner. You use your experience and interests, a knowledge of convention and taste, of individuals' preferences. You might work it out on paper, checking the ingredients you have or you know you can get. You might adventurously try cooking a dish you've never done before. And throughout – and afterwards – you'll reappraise what you've done to make it as good or better next time. Do likewise with your home.

Buy authentic

I don't mean 'authentic' Levi jeans, I mean stuff that is made in the firm's own factories, where they look after the people they employ and the place where they're based (this idea is the antithesis of 'brand' as expressed above). Alessi make kitchenware from steel and plastics (not bamboo and hemp) but they score highly in my view because they're still a family-run business working out of the same town in Italy. So do EcoForce plastic products, a British firm who produce clothes pegs, pan scourers and sponges out of recycled waste in their factory in Wellingborough.

These companies are easy to research on the web and they're generally not multinationals like Eon or Ford: they're rooted in a place and a community and that makes them worth supporting. Not that you should buy things that you don't need or love just because you like the company. A crucial maxim of buying authentically is that written by the 19th-century writer and craftsman William Morris: 'If you want a golden rule that will fit everything, this is it: Have nothing in your houses that you do not know to be useful or believe to be beautiful.

Bag some game

Buy food instead of clothes and household goods. Make the shopping adventure a hunt for locally reared herb-fed lamb or some organic free-range tomatoes. Treat yourself twice this way, because unlike the pair of shoes that never gets worn, you'll probably get round to eating your purchase in the next week.

Buy the autobiographical

What the hell does that mean? What it says. The vase that has a piece of paper in it telling you who the maker is and when and how it was made already has a story attached to it, a narrative. And I promise you that you will have a richer, more enjoyable relationship with an object when you know its story. The diffusion 'branded' vase or the cheap one from the market is a bit hollow by comparison.

If you need a trophy, make it a trophy...

for the hours of bargain-hunting. Make it something that you can appreciate day in, day out, and develop a relationship with. Make it something small, inexpensive, comfortable, functional and beautiful. Like a cushion.

Chapter Thirteen
THINGS AT HOME WORTH INVESTING IN

Touch is a much underrated sense. Whether you're a child in a toyshop or an adult in a china shop, or you're in bed with your lover, the temptation to touch is too great to resist.

Retailers place the emphasis on the visual: we're encouraged to look but not touch, and window displays are kept out of reach behind glass. Yet the tactile – being able to touch, hold, stroke and grip things – is fundamental to our full experience of the world around us. If you ask any architect where the money on a project should go, they will tell you that it's worth investing in 1) the bare bones of the design and a good quality of construction and 2) the things you touch.

We can all tell the difference between a door handle that wobbles and one made with a firm spring and a satisfying 'action'. Thanks to ergonomic car design, we can all appreciate the firm 'clunk' of a door closing – from both the sound and the feel of it. A stainless-steel stair handrail will feel uncomfortable and mean if it has bumpy welds or sharp edges, whereas it'll make you want to stroke it if it is beautifully finished and sandy smooth. So, because you touch them everyday, here's a list of things worth investing in.

Choose the architecture, garden, decoration and furnishings around who you are, what you dream of and what has made you. The most interesting and enriching homes are those that are full of autobiography; those that are maybe a bit cluttered, feel lived in and are delightful for it; those that have a mix of new and old, borrowed and bought – and not those that resemble furniture showrooms. A home is not a shop.

PROPER FURNITURE

I don't mean this in the way your dowager aunt might in dismissing anything designed after 1915. I mean furniture that is made with love and care. It is probably going to be expensive but it will reward you, I promise, in the fullness of time with a longer life and more use and somehow a livelier character, because you know it well and the factory it came from and maybe even the person who made it, thanks to a little brochure that came with the furniture that you may end up keeping as long as the furniture.

It may sound soppy and sentimental, but I know it to be fact that if a thing is made with love, chances are you will end up loving it. And stroking it now and again. I know this because when I used to run a crafts-based manufacturing business, making lighting and furniture, the heart of the business was the forge where three men, Norman, Richard and Steve, would sweat and toil for some money, some overtime and the simple

love of what they did. They were all master craftsmen at the very top of their game, winning prizes in competitions at the weekends, for whom hammering bits of hot metal was pure joy. Clients would often write to thank the entire company for turning out a bespoke table or a chandelier and these letters would get grubbily passed around and avidly read, closing the loop, as it were, of commitment and passion, feeding a love of the object back to the people who made it. This virtuous circle, where the object was no longer a lifeless thing but an appreciated and understood vehicle for the human energy and commitment that went into making it, would be most felt when a client visited the forge, often to be told that

Richard or Norman had spent a month or so of their lives making this or that unique item for them. Clients were often stunned into silent admiration for the time and effort required just to make something, but the most touching moments always came after they had left, when I saw big hairy men with hammers moved to tears by the experience of being thanked.

Ever since, I've thought of every decently made object I've seen or picked up, from lamp posts and bridges to spoons and eggcups, as not just 'stuff' but a physical embodiment of human energy: the magical ability of our species to take raw materials and turn them into things of use, value and beauty. It's why I wrote this book.

66 **Stands to reason that anything you sit on and anything you plonk your elbows on wants to be a good surface.** 99

LIGHT SWITCHES & TABLE LAMPS

The action of something like a light switch should not only feel crisp and easy, it should feel the same way thousands of uses later. This is down to the quality of the components (the rocker, steel spring) and the quality of the assembly. In the case of lighting, we're used nowadays to being able to buy a bedside lamp for around £5 in a DIY store. But because it's cheap, that doesn't mean to say it's disposable or planet-light. The environmental impact of lighting is heavy, because each fixture comprises many components from many materials that have travelled many thousands of miles before being assembled. The average bedside lamp might contain five separate types of plastic, a spun aluminium shade, brass and steel components, PVC cabling, copper wire, silicone gaskets, rubber sheathing, ceramic lampholder and fuse; and, in

the bulb, rare gases, glass, tungsten or (if it's a compact fluorescent) rare metal phosphors, mercury, electronic components and a circuit board.

That is such a lot of resources from all over the globe, condensed into one tiny purchase. And that price is only possible because there is an unseen backwash of costs that are hidden, or banked for future generations to incur, in the wider environment. The mercury will have an associated cost for it to be extracted in the recycling process. The cost of cleaning up the rivers around the world's copper mines and compensating local villagers and workers alike for health problems will run to tens of millions. The PVC cable will have been made in a factory where cancer risk is high because of the amount of toxins locally released into the

atmosphere, dioxin being a significant by-product of PVC manufacture and its disposal. As it sits in your bedroom, the PVC cable is slowly leaching plasticizers like phthalates into the atmosphere. The chlorine from the PVC (comprising 57 per cent of its mass) will leach from landfill into watercourses and poison wildlife. You get a lot of significant environmental impact for £5, don't you?

So my advice is, whether you spend £5 or £300 on a table lamp, buy it with the intention of keeping it for ever. Don't think of it as disposable, because in truth it isn't. It will carry on having an effect on the planet and human health long after you've thrown it out. Don't think of it as recyclable because it isn't, not fully. Many plastics are not ground up and recycled in the West because it's not economic to do so. Think of it as something to cherish.

TAPS

They light up, they dispense water when you wave your hands in front of them, they disgorge water in all kinds of fancy ways, but there are only five important things about taps.

1. **They shouldn't wobble.**
2. **They shouldn't fall apart or drip.**
3. **If there are indices, marked 'Hot' and 'Cold', they shouldn't wear off.**
4. **The action and the surface should feel good.**
5. **They should be sustainably made. Engineering like this is energy intensive and for taps to be vaguely ecological they should be made from recycled brass, be recyclable, use closed-loop plating processes and be made in the country of consumption.**

YOUR ENTIRE BATHROOM

Bathing is a sensuous experience and even washing and shaving can be pleasures with the right materials around you. An acrylic bath may hold the heat longer than an enamelled-steel or cast-iron equivalent, but it just doesn't feel as good. On the other hand, knowing that your bare flesh has been in contact with stone tiles quarried in some mine by underpaid, under-age labour in India or China can make you feel dirty rather than clean. The rule in researching surfaces and finishes for your home has to be 'shop local', in other words from within your country and only then further afield. Don't stray from your continent and remember that just because you find a French stone company which cuts onyx, that doesn't mean the onyx is from France.

STAIR HANDRAILS

Really important because we don't just touch them but also move our hands over them. Consequently, any little inconsistency can make itself obvious. A sensuously flowing, flawless and tactile handrail can also make up for any amount of clumsiness in the design of the staircase itself. Believe me, the experience you remember is the one you touch.

ABOVE: A GLASSeco kitchen worktop, made from recycled glass and set in resin

PRINCIPLE
30

Every decently made object, from a house to a lamp post to a bridge, spoon or eggcup, is not just a piece of 'stuff' but a physical embodiment of human energy, testimony to the magical ability of our species to take raw materials and turn them into things of use, value and beauty.

KITCHEN WORKTOPS

On this one surface you're likely to prepare your food for the next ten years, make tea and even make love if your life's racy enough. It's got to be sanitary, durable and tactile. I don't recommend timber, because although it's tactile, the surface will probably stain with time and harbour microbes. And there's a chance you'll get splinters. I can recommend stone and granite – providing it's not shipped halfway round the planet just for your delectation – and stainless steel and resin. When I say resin I don't mean 100 per cent petroleum-derived plastic but one of the brands made with either crushed waste granite quartz or crushed car windscreens that are then bound with around 10 per cent resin. They are hard and long lasting, and can be moulded to almost any form.

DOOR HANDLES

After everything I've written here already about the satisfaction of using well-made, properly engineeered, sustainable goods, it should be obvious why you should invest in high-quality door furniture – for everything from cupboards to drawers to the front door.

CUTLERY, GLASS WARE, IMPLEMENTS AND CROCKERY

The most sensorily developed parts of our bodies are our mouths and our fingertips. In other words, the two places where we put our forks and spoons. Note coincidentally, the last resting place of high-quality materials in the modern world is the restaurant, where you'll come into contact with linen, horsehair fabric, bone-handled silver, porcelain, crystal glass and hopefully some of the same high quality food. Any good restaurateur knows the value of these materials in enriching the experience of eating well and this is a good lesson to take home. Even if you never buy outrageously expensive designer crockery, go to a good shop and get them to explain how a proper knife balances in the hand. It's enlightening.

PRINCIPLE
31

The most interesting homes are those that do the architectural thing of embodying the spirit of a place and time and the very architectural thing of reflecting the people who live there.

SO HOW ABOUT THIS FOR FIRST PRINCIPLES?

A campaign to reintroduce tactility and encourage people to buy the real thing. Metal pens for a start and furniture that's made from real solid wood and upholstered with horsehair or silk or proper leather. Also vintage mahogany toilet seats. And if possible, a mobile phone made from burr walnut with mother-of-pearl inlay and a knitted woollen case.

It's not going to work, is it? Because there isn't enough burr walnut on the planet to make a mobile phone for every adult on the planet.

And if there were enough, chopping down the trees wouldn't make sense. Meanwhile, there is enough plastic spewing out of oil refineries – often as a by-product of fuel production – to make a mobile phone for every man, woman and child. I can only suggest you get yourself a little mobile 'sock' knitted out of possum fur, possum being an official 'pest' and therefore ethically transformable into fur products.

And as you might do when food shopping, go local – or at least regional – and go organic.

CAR

This is going to sound heretical, but why not choose a car on the basis of what it looks and feels like on the inside? Given that is where you're going to be spending your time and that's the place where you'll develop your relationship with the thing, it's perfectly reasonable to demand an interesting environment. My own baby Volvo has seats made of reasonably ecological leather and a beautifully designed floating centre console. Of course there's too much plastic but there's also wool and a smattering of recycled aluminium to stroke. And my car rewards me with 65 miles to the gallon, a miserly consumption that adds to the pleasure of driving it. As to the exterior – well, it just needs a wash.

MAC OR PC?

Mac owners will gloat at this point. Cleaning the aluminium case of my own little Apple is no chore but an act of caring, like stroking a Furby. I won't admit to it being fetishistic but it's a little like wax polishing a fine old piece of French polished furniture. OK, that's enough, I'm sure, for all you PC owners trying to remove the crumbs from your keyboard. I will just add that using a Mac is a tactile pleasure and an intellectual one too. With a PC, not only does all that plastic get scratched, worn and dirty, but even trying to operate the software feels a bit dirty in comparison. Yuk.

32

Buy the auto-biographical. The vase that has a piece of paper in it telling you who the maker is and when and how it was made already has a story attached to it, a narrative. You will have a richer, more enjoyable relationship with an object when you know its story.

BEDDING

Bet you didn't expect to find this on the list. But I'm assuming you sleep in cotton sheets, or polycotton if you're a bachelor. And I need to put you off cotton. Why? Well, in a newly bought 100-per-cent-cotton bedsheet or pillowcase there is only 73 per cent cotton, the rest being chemicals added to the fabric during growing or treatment, including formaldehyde. Not that this is the worst chemical you'll be sleeping on: Aldicarb, Parathion and Methamidophos are in the top ten insecticide treatments for cotton crops (used extensively all over the world, including the United States) and are three of the most acutely hazardous chemicals listed by the World Health Organization. Indeed, according to the Environmental Protection Agency, 7 out of the top 15 chemicals used on cotton are 'possible', 'known', 'likely' or 'probable' human carcinogens. Others are hormone disruptors and toxic in other ways.

Of the world's cultivated land, 2.5 per cent is given over to cotton and yet it consumes 25 per cent of insecticides used. In the US alone, that's 25,000 tonnes every year. For every kilo of raw cotton (enough for a couple of T-shirts), the plant uses a kilo of synthetic nitrogen fertilizer, which produces N2O, a greenhouse gas 300 times more potent than carbon dioxide. Cottonseed hulls are sold for animal feeds, so that 65 per cent of cotton production ends up in our food chain. In Third World countries, health among cotton farmers is poor and pesticide use often unregulated. Still want to spend a third of your life lying on this stuff?

Meanwhile, organic cotton production is mercilessly free of such evils. So buy organic bedclothes. Or go one better and buy the fabric made from flax that needs, even when farmed intensively, five times less pesticide and fertilizer, and no chemical treatments: linen. Linen, when washed, becomes extraordinarily soft to the touch, it is an experience to sleep on it and, unlike cotton, it keeps you warm in winter and cool in summer. Like cotton, it is also grown organically.

CLOTHES

I thought I should add 'clothes' because for the time you're not sleeping in fabric, you're pretty well surrounded by it. The same arguments apply as above, although issues of taste, colour, fashion and tradition cloud our decision-making when we buy clothes. So all I'll offer is the briefest of personal lists. I, like everyone, do not like my clothes to be exclusively hand-woven from free-range Fairtrade sackcloth. I prefer my jeans to be organic cotton or hemp (jeans – from Nimes in France, hence the word 'denims' – were originally woven from hemp fibre), dyed with natural dyes. I don't buy plastic clothes other than for going up mountains in and filming outdoors. I buy T-shirts made from organic cotton and I wear a lot of tops and T-shirts woven from the genius fabric that is merino wool that never smells. Hmmm. I like natural fibres and I like to know that they're chemical free. It's also comforting when I know that my underpants weren't sewn together by near-slave labour in Turkey. But I can never be sure.

Chapter Fourteen

THINGS AT HOME NOT WORTH INVESTING IN

William Morris, the 19th-century writer and craftsman, reminded us all that the simple pleasures of domestic life hold more for us than any home entertainment system when he wrote: 'Simplicity of life, even the barest, is not a misery, but the very foundation of refinement; a sanded floor and whitewashed walls and the green trees, and flowery meads, and living waters outside.'

Let's face it, though, it takes more than a flowery mead to occupy us for a Saturday afternoon these days. The Energy Savings Trust produced a report in 2006 called The Rise of the Machines comparing our dependence on appliances in the 1970s, when home entertainment consisted of a hi-fi, television, transistor radio and cassette recorder (plus, I remember, Airfix model making and macramé), with that in the 21st-century. Nowadays, the number of leisure machines has grown from the statutory four to maybe a couple of dozen in the average household, from iPod and mobile phone to satellite TV boxes, home computers, and a telly and mini hi-fi in every other room. However, I should add that music has not got any better and television has got worse.

The net effect of all this technology is the consumption of more energy. We use twice as much electricity at home now as we did in the 1970s and the amount is still rising, not least because the average household has 12 gadgets on standby at any point. In total, appliances left on standby in the UK consume about two power stations' worth of fuel. Crazy.

It seems clear that we could be perfectly happy with less stuff around us. Indeed, as Oxford professor Avner Offer points out, although there is an identified link between a rise in material standard of living and a rise in happiness and sense of well-being since the Second World War, we could have achieved the same rise in happiness with much less material growth.

I certainly don't think my household is any less happy for only having one TV and just two hi-fis – both of which are 20 years old. With the rise of brand, the fashion for technology and the lust for walk-in fridges (which together with large, fuel-hungry range cookers have become the Range Rovers of interior design) the last 40 years have also witnessed an unpalatable change in the way we view our homes, not as personal statements, where thrift, character and autobiography matter, but as statements of luxury.

Meanwhile, the things we considered luxuries 40 years ago are now seen as basic rights as our patterns of consumption swell, it seems inexorably. Despite the economic crisis of 2008–9 producing an interest in the ownership of small, lean cars, the number of cars on British roads with an engine size of more than 2 litres has doubled from around 2 million in 1999 to 4 million in early 2010, according to the Office for National Statistics. Meanwhile, there has been continued growth in the number of households with access to two or more cars, from around 2 per cent in the 1950s to more than 30 per cent in 2008. The number of journeys made by public transport has risen slightly since the 1990s from around 6 to 7 billion, but is still well below the 12 billion figure of the 1960s.

The standard 21st-century act of affluence is to be seen to be throwing money away, conspicuously consuming material goods like fuel and indeed cars themselves. In terms of our dwellings, such high-profile consumption means buying a beautiful old house as a display of wealth. Old houses are charming and desirable for their 'character' — something that is usually down to the lightness of touch that previous owners have exercised in looking after an old place, so that it feels accretive and interesting for its layers of history, the thrifty way it has been added to and repaired, and the deep sense of autobiography that it expresses in a thousand tiny details.

The act of affluence, however, is to rip all this out as quickly as possible, eliminating all traces of thrift, autobiography and character to install underheated polished limestone floors, downlighters, smooth new walls and a walk-in fridge. This is putting a brand-new show-off house inside an ancient show-off shell. It's now only a matter of time before owners of these grim, moribund homes knock out the 18th-century French doors to be able to park their Range Rover Sport in the kitchen.

Enough ranting. To help you avoid an addiction to luxury for its own sake and to help you save money and carbon, these are the things you do not need to spend money on.

PRINCIPLE

Make everything you touch of the very highest quality. Door handles, locks, switches, chairs and controls should be an ergonomic pleasure to use and robust enough for that pleasure to continue.

THE FORMAL DINING ROOM

When did you last have a formal dinner party? How many do you throw a month? Or every decade, for that matter?

The traditional arrangement of houses in the western hemisphere is to organize rooms around separate activities: reading books, sleeping, cooking, eating. And much of that organization implied domestic servants to arrange those activities. In the mid-1980s I reorganized a home for a client who lived in a standard terraced house – the kind anyone reading this book would recognize – that was laid out in the 1880s with a front room, a dining room (both had been knocked together) and a separate kitchen at the back of the house. The kitchen was placed there out of tradition but also expediency, because the original developer was able to run the services like water and drainage along the alley that ran between the backs of the housing terraces to feed the outside toilets and kitchens.

We swapped everything around to suit the informality of modern life. No dining room, no sitting room, just a big social space with the kitchen at the front of the house near the front door (making it easily accessible for shopping, waste and recycling movements). Despite the tininess of the house, this room was big enough for a dining table, television and sofa too, along the lines of the traditional informal farmhouse kitchen, where food preparation, socializing and informal leisure all take place together. Meanwhile, the old kitchen was adapted with a large picture window overlooking the garden (including the spot where the old outside khazi had once stood), hi-fi, sofa, desk and books, as a place for contemplation, study and screen-free relaxation.

When you plan the layout of your home, do it around the way you live, not how you fantasize you might one day live.

KITCHEN CUPBOARDS AND DOORS

The bits that matter in the kitchen are the machines that do the work and the bits you come into contact with. Look at Chapter 13 and you'll see these include door handles, taps and worktops. Knives and pans are also important. But door cupboards aren't. And frankly, the best-made kitchens in the world are still 'carcassed out' using orientated strand board, chipboard or plywood. Structurally, there's a negligible difference in quality between the £5,000 kitchen and its £50,000 equivalent. Moreover, high-street merchants like Ikea have got wise to this and are now retailing budget kit kitchens that mimic the bespoke German ones. It also seems daft to spend vast quantities on an aspect of your home that the next owners will invariably rip out and replace. Which they will, because it's human nature to territorialise the new cave with a new kitchen. All of which demands that you invest in kitchen units and doors that are ecological, recyclable and for that matter probably recycled in the first place, from a company like Chamois Kitchens.

THE 500-SQUARE-FOOT SITTING ROOM

I have spent the last twelve years of my life making programmes about people building houses that are, in the main, too big. It's generally true that when people build their own home they're doing so to provide themselves and their family with more space, a more customized home and a more intelligent and efficient building. But these places need to be efficient, super-insulated and fuel miserly because often they're vast. We don't need big houses, we just like them. We relish the luxury of space and height but these – volume – a lot of air to heat and cool; and a lot of raw materials to go into the structure too. The most nonsensical eco-houses I've come across are the big ones. In fact they can't rightfully be called eco-houses.

So let me redefine the luxury of space. Having spent a third of my time over the last few years living with my family in a 750-square-foot apartment I can tell you that the most luxurious space/volume you can own is a cupboard. Proper, clever storage, built into a building, is a miracle space-saving measure, allowing the habitable areas to be clutter free and feel, well, spacious. So before you start to plan that ambitious self-build, buy a catalogue of 'storage solution' shelving.

> **66 We don't need big houses, we just like them. We relish the luxury of space and height. 99**

THE NEW

Human beings have an odd fascination for the new. It's not just that as individuals we succumb to the odd new iPod or car; companies, city councils and national governments also miraculously fall prey to the idea that the next new thing will solve all their woes. This explains why historic neighbourhoods are torn down to make way for a new plaza, why we have a culture where buildings are destroyed rather than adapted and

repaired, and why the British National Health Service has so far spent £12.7 billion on an IT system that is at least five years late in completion and which a mere 160 health organizations out of 9,000 in the country use properly.

This kind of cock-up isn't unique to Britain because secure computer systems take a very long while to install and network across a country, and so by the time a system's finished, it's obsolete. Constant

updating and renewal become a major 'on-cost'. Architecture works in a similar way, because by the time a building is complete, its design is already out of date. The great Rem Koolhaus has complained that the design and planning process can take so many years that there is no chance of architecture reflecting the mood of an age.

And what an age: a new century looking for a new expression and identity to

reflect our post-industrial, post-modern, postage-stamp mentality. All we can satisfy ourselves with is that any new building is shiny and clean. In fact it is remarkable just how vulnerable we all, and I include you and me and our government here, are to the glittery persuasiveness of the bling. A great number of new buildings are covered in glass, or ceramic or shiny metal, the construction equivalents of sweet wrappers. Perhaps, in

taking cues from half a century of supermarket shopping, the best style we can come up with for a new millennium is one based on packaging.

So if you take my advice you won't rush to embrace the New right now. I once interviewed a lady living in a mock-period new-built house about why she liked it. Her answer was, 'Why would I buy something that looked absolutely modern? In five years' time it'll look out of

date.' She was insuring herself against superannuation.

If you own something old – a house, a chair, a lawnmower – don't chuck it; instead, repair it, use it and think of it as a backdrop to the occasional newer thing. That worn paint and not-so-shiny surface has more character and relevance to the 'now' than a piece of shiny plastic, because its surface tells a story that leads right up to the present moment.

THE WALK-IN FRIDGE

Obviously the only walk-in fridges you'll find are in restaurant kitchens and cold-storage facilities. I'm talking about American-style giant fridge freezers, the width of two first-class extra-fatty airline seats, fridges that cost anything between £500 and £8,000. The kind that make you ice, chill your champagne to 4.76°C and produce year round snow for novelty dinner parties.

Despite many of them achieving an 'A' rating for power efficiency or (in the US) an Energy Star efficiency mark, this is only for best in class: most of them consume over 500 kilowatt hours per year of electricity, the largest as much as 700kWh per year.

According to the US EPA Energy Star website, automatic ice-makers and through-the-door dispensers also increase energy use by 14–20 per cent. These are behemoths of fuel consumption and unless you're a gamekeeper who needs to chill a quartered stag every other week, I can't understand why any family truly needs one.

In *How to Live a Low-Carbon Life*, Chris Goodall gives a rule of thumb. Look for a fridge of around 300 litres in size, that uses 300kWh of electricity a year and that costs under £300. And I say, if you can, build a ventilated larder, a cold room in which to keep salads, preserves and juices.

THE FANCY COOKER

Fancy Cooker Syndrome is a domestic extension of Shiny Car Syndrome. Just as the Shiny Car gets you across a city at the same average 11mph as a fibreglass electric car (or, as it happens, a horse and cart did in London in 1911), so the Fancy Cooker will make hot food no better and no more quickly than an old enamel Belling out of a skip. Until 2001 I owned a white enamel Belling cooker that came out of a skip. Only two out of three rings worked and the oven had one setting only – on. Yet this majestic warhorse provided not just hot food but fantastic cuisine for family and friends.

I can understand why you might want a shiny car: it makes you look more beautiful/increases your manhood and it might offer a pleasant environment in which to travel across London at 11mph. But the cooker doesn't do either of these. It doesn't do anything other than cook food. In fact it's so stupid it doesn't even do that, because people cook food. Put an expensive casserole in the Fancy Cooker, turn it on and sooner or later the casserole will just catch fire.

BATHROOMS AND POWER SHOWERS

Despite the fact that they get ripped out, I can't counsel you to buy a cheapo bathroom because it's the one place where you regularly come into contact with the surfaces. A great deal of you, in fact, with a great deal of it. Invest in good fittings with flow regulators and aerators to conserve water. If anything, make sure the tiles can be easily replaced without damaging the sanitary ware. That should keep the new owners happy.

Time was when a man could take a shower and emerge feeling so beaten up he had to go back to bed. Manufacturers are now wising up to the fact that it's possible to deliver a really enjoyable shower without consuming Wales's average national rainfall and leaving you with the sensation that you've been power-hammered into the bathroom floor. Through technologies like pulsing and aerating the water (be careful here because the water can be so aerated that it can leave the shower head hot but hit you lukewarm) the amount of water used can be drastically reduced. This is becoming increasingly important because our water consumption has more than doubled since the 1970s to 150 litres per person per day. Water is going to become a scarcer resource with a burgeoning population and an increasingly undependable climate.

MEDIA ROOM

I know that just now I suggested designing your home around your way of life, and that may include a wealth of media. So why not organize a room dedicated to music, gaming, Internet chat, porntube and iPod apps?

What a good idea. My answer is one based on pure prejudice. When I look at plans of a new home and see the words 'home cinema', 'Pilates room' and 'media centre', I sigh. I like the words 'study' and 'library' because I like books. Sorry.

AND A FEW THINGS NOT TO PUT INTO YOUR HOUSE

Today, candles are made with synthetic materials and perfumes that give off carbon monoxide and volatile organic compounds. In fact, our homes are now miniature chemical warehouses, stocked with poisons and noxious materials and our furniture and carpets are held together with formaldehyde and phthalates – hormone-disrupting chemicals. If you want to breathe fresh air, go and stand on a motorway bridge. In the meantime, here is some sobering information on the chemical products that can be found in your home.

Formaldehyde

Formaldehyde is used in glues, adhesives, paints and pressed wood products. It has a pungent smell and can cause watery eyes, breathing difficulties, nausea, and burning sensations in the eyes and throat. High concentrations can trigger asthma attacks. It has also been shown to cause cancer in animals and it may cause cancer in humans.

In the 1970s, many homeowners had urea-formaldehyde foam insulation installed in wall cavities as an energy conservation measure, but many of these homes were found to have high indoor concentrations of formaldehyde, and few houses are now insulated this way.

Other volatile organic compounds

Formaldehyde belongs to a group of liquids and gases called VOCs which vaporize at room temperature and react with other pollutants to form ozone. High concentrations of ozone harm human health, damage crops, and contribute to global warming and the destruction of the stratospheric ozone shield that protects the earth's surface from harmful ultra-violet radiation. VOCs are found in paints, glues, solvents, aerosol sprays, construction products, fabrics, wallpaper and plastics. Concentrations of VOCs are up to ten times higher indoors than outdoors and unwelcome health effects include eye and respiratory tract irritation, headaches, dizziness, visual disorders and memory impairment.

PVC

Polyvinyl chloride (PVC) is used in pipelines, wiring, cladding, flooring and wallpaper. It is cheap and easy to install, but has high environmental and health costs. PVC releases dioxin and other organic pollutants during its manufacture and recycling is difficult because of its high chlorine content. There are safer alternatives for virtually all PVC applications, using sustainable materials — such as wood, and terracotta. PVC can also be replaced by bio-plastics that can be made from raw natural materials such as starch and cellulose.

Phthalates – in carpets and plastics

Phthalates are chemicals added to common consumer products as vinyl softening agents. Humans are widely exposed to phthalates because vinyl is a ubiquitous plastic used to make anything from home furnishings and medical devices to infant's feeding bottles and food wrap. We're also exposed to phthalates in the form of perfumes, soaps, lotions and shampoos. Phthalates are also added to insecticides, adhesives, sealants and car-care products. In 1999, prompted by the potential of babies to intake dangerous amounts of phthalates, the EU placed an emergency ban on the use of certain phthalates in toys made for children under the age of three. This emergency ban was renewed in 2005.

Copper-chrome-arsenic-treated timber

Chromated copper arsenate (CCA) is a highly toxic wood preservative made from copper, chromium and arsenic, which is now banned. Because it was so effective there are still millions of tonnes of timber extant that have been treated with CCA, such as fencing, cladding, and roofing. It can be recognized by the greenish tint it gives timber. Scrap CCA timber continues to be widely burnt through ignorance, and it is a serious risk if burnt in confined spaces.

You should always handle CCA-treated wood outdoors, wearing a dust mask, goggles and gloves – and you must never mulch or compost it.

Spores, moulds and mushrooms

Our homes contain hundreds of contaminants from living organisms. Bacteria, viruses, dust mites, animal dander and moulds can all be more pernicious than chemical products in your kitchen cupboard. Moulds, in particular, can thrive in damp houses or on moist window frames, causing serious respiratory and digestive tract problems. So always keep your house well ventilated and if you have a heat-recovery system, check the heat exchanger regularly for damp and mould.

Endangered species

Our increasing consumption of palm oil for food and fuel has directly led to the threatened extinction of orang-utans in South-East Asia, with their populations reduced by 30 per cent in just ten years. This is to keep you and me in fast food and biofuels. Coltan mining, meanwhile, has decimated Africa's gorilla population, because of our demand for new mobile phones. The Asian elephant is under threat from logging, agriculture, and road building.

It doesn't take only something as ostentatious as a fur rug to threaten a species. In fact, if you see an old tiger skin for sale second-hand, buy it and use it as a reminder of the effect we are having on the natural environment every time we buy fuel, food, clothes or luxury goods.

Chapter Fifteen
PATINA

Once you accept that there is no such thing as 'new', that even your plastic-wrapped just-bought mobile phone was manufactured last year and packaged seven months ago and that its replacement which looks even cooler is already in production for release next year, then you start getting interested in the old. Old is the stuff you bought yesterday and the stuff you bought last year and the stuff your grandfather bought in 1937 and gave you wrapped in waxed paper.

The new thing starts to age the moment it is made. True, you can take ownership of a phone and make it your own by downloading some new apps, personalizing a wallpaper and pushing the oil from your very own fingers all over its keyboard and screen. That may make it newly yours, but not new. (Years ago, kids took ownership of books by scrawling their names all over the covers. Graffiti is a time-honoured expression of ownership of things and, for that matter, connection to a place, whether it's a street wall or a school desk.)

It's curious that at one extreme of the design scale there exists an obsession with the idea of the ultra-new, ultra-clean (think design anoraks who obsess over white leather floors and faultless, clutterless symmetry in their homes), whilst at the other collector anoraks of classical art and antiques pursue the most sought-after patinas on ancient bronze sculptures. They're looking for dirt, oxidation and the waxy oil finish that generations of fingers have left behind.

These things – dirt, oxidation and human grease – are the enemies of good skincare, we're told. They're what give you spots. But they are the ne plus ultra of bronze sculpture; modern-day artists who cast in bronze pursue the finishing of their work with the same obsession as the classicists. There are encyclopedias of metal finishing that offer hundreds of different colours for the patination of brass, copper, bronze and silver, from deep reds to lustrous pinks and the crusty weather-worn verdigris of 2,000-year-old bronzework. I've even written books on how to achieve these effects with paint – how to fake the distressing, antiquing effects of age. I was a very young man when I wrote those books, and now that age and the antique are distressingly advancing, I prefer to embrace the clean and white a little more.

But there is no doubt that bronze in particular is a material that we not only accept as looking old and mottled but demand it looks so, even when the material is freshly minted. I suspect that's because we know and accept the fact that even when patinated with the effects of time, a bronze sculpture will last intact for thousands of years. Age shall not wither it.

We're a lot less accepting of our pride-and-joy ten-year-old car turning to rust. That's because rust is not a surface patination, like verdigris. It's the wholesale attack of the atmosphere on our assets that pretty soon will crumble to a pile of red dust if we don't get out the sandpaper and red primer paint. The rusting of steel – in our cars, buildings and bridges – represents a threat to our built environment, just as the slow surface patination of a sculpture, copper roof or old piece of furniture is an enhancement of it.

I needn't explain the obvious about how plastics become brittle, crack and deteriorate with time. This happens so quickly that unless you're three years old you'll have seen evidence of this in your own home. I should point out, though, that much 'patination' and 'oxidation' is simply the refined material, be it steel, aluminium or polyethylene, attempting to right the natural wrong of finding itself in an artificially pure state and responding by trying to return to its natural state. Timber, once cut and no longer part of a tree, will usually, when dampened, hurry to disintegrate into its raw elemental materials with the help of fungi and beetles. Iron and steel rust in an attempt to revert to iron ores such as haematite, which for all the world look, in the natural environment, like lumps of rust; my 1988 IBM computer case has turned a deep ghoulish yellow as it tries to return to its primeval roots – I fully expect it to melt into a sticky pool of crude oil within the decade. These materials are wilful.

The trouble is that the vast majority of the world is built out of timber, steel and plastic, meaning that no matter how hard we try, that world has a built-in obsolescence. Of course there are a few, noble materials such as gold and palladium which do not degrade, but they are also not so common and not so interesting for engineers as steel. Aluminium, once refined, is remarkably stable, forming a white dusty oxide on its surface which helps to protect the pure metal beneath. Then there are those stuffs that have some resistance to the ravages of the world: bronze, stainless steel, glass, ceramics, polished marbles. These are materials that we value for their longevity and often pay a lot of cash to have in our lives. The obvious extensions to this list are the marbles and stones of extreme durability and resistance to tarnishing that we put on our fingers: the agates, rubies, emeralds, sapphires and diamonds that will outlast us and all the bronze in the world.

Without providing a list that Nero would have demanded for his palace, here are some materials that will offer you a great deal of lasting pleasure in your home as you enjoy watching and feeling them age – usually more slowly than you do.

LASTING PLEASURE

Bronze

Enough said about this material, save that you can buy door handles and table legs cast from this durable – and expensive – metal, which is an alloy of tin and copper. The hundreds of patinae that this material will develop or chemically take are all lively and interesting.

Brass...

is cheaper but a younger invention, there being no 'brass age'. The Romans minted coins from brass (an alloy of copper and zinc) and enjoyed its gold-like colour, but production was always limited because of the difficulties of obtaining zinc from calamine, a mineral. Historically, then, this was the more exotic alloy, used in 18th-century clockmaking, but early 19th-century production techniques enabled its mass production. The average nickel or chrome handle or tap will probably be cast from brass, not bronze, or hot 'sintered' (a form of cooler, pressurized casting) from brass powder. Brass is a metal that, unlike

bronze or copper, looks duller and less interesting with age. On the other hand, when hand-polished (not lacquered, which can make it look sticky), brass can appear bright and almost silvery, with little yellow colour, as the zinc is brought out. It's time intensive to look after, but rewarding if polished regularly.

Lead

That heavy old metal has a lumpy appeal about it and a greyish dull weathered patina. Apart from car batteries and use as a radiation shield, it's nowadays seen only on and around old buildings, where it is worked as a roofing material that is usually highly crafted – on church roofs in sheets and around chimneys and gable ends as waterproofing 'flashing'. It has also for thousands of years been employed as a damp proof course, for sealing joints in masonry, setting iron into stone, glazing windows, constructing and lining water cisterns, and making water pipes. The Romans considered the finest lead in the empire

to come from the Mendip Hills in Somerset, the hills on which I live and which are still scarred with the bumps and hollows of ancient lead workings. Among the old stone farmhouses and city terraces of nearby Bath, no historic house seems complete without lead flashings on the roof or a finely wrought glazing came of leadwork. And it is infinitely recyclable, with a melting point of around 330°C. But it is also extremely toxic, and just a few days' exposure to lead dust (say from grinding it) can damage the central nervous system, blood system or kidneys permanently. Lead-based oil paints were used until a few decades ago as the standard coating for timber, and so you should never sandpaper these paints back but instead chemically strip them. Lead, thank God, is not nowadays considered appropriate for water pipes, although old water pipes were so encrusted on the inside with lead carbonate, precipitated out of the chalk or lime in the water, that very little lead made it into the water.

PRINCIPLE
34

Allow things to patinate. Do not jettison the things you own because they become tired. Accept the character that time confers and that the moment something is newly made, it starts to become old.

Pewter...

is the acceptable face of lead. A similar colour, with a propensity to darken with age to a warm brownish grey, traditional cheap pewter used lead combined with antimony, bismuth and copper to form an alloy which could be spun, cast, soldered and engraved. English pewter was traditionally made with over 90 per cent tin, and since 1974 lead has been banned from the mix. Just as lead was never introduced into the home, its proper place being outside on the building, so pewter served as the raw material for high-class plates, goblets, bowls and dishes until porcelain manufacture and advancements in glassmaking in the 18th century. Any modern reproduction pewter will be of relatively low toxicity compared to historical examples – although I wouldn't go so far as to eat off the stuff – and it's a shame that more contemporary design isn't executed in this soft, charming material.

Glass & crystal...

are simple to make, from basic raw materials like soda, ash and sand, and they've been in production for around 3,000 years. And yet their transparency and perfection set them apart from other materials that are forged out of the earth. The Venetians were the first, around 1500, to remove the metals such as iron and copper which tinted glass and produce colourless cristallo, although it was George Ravenscroft at the end of the 17th century in England who developed methods of adding lead oxide to form lead crystal.

189

PART FOUR

SHA

RING

Chapter Sixteen

SHARING OUT THE GARBAGE

One of the founding principles of Hab was that we would work with communities to produce something approaching 'social architecture'; we want to be developers who don't just build houses up to the red line that marks the edge of our plot; we want to construct homes and make places that new residents will want to buy and existing surrounding residents would like too.

We want to create community land trusts so that residents can take ownership of the public realm around them and so that the red line becomes fuzzy. A simple example of this is where a new community runs its own car club, play equipment and kitchen gardens but shares these with the people who live in the surrounding neighbourhood.

But I am a developer nevertheless and the suspicion (nay, the empirical evidence) is that developers don't care. Because planning law in the UK makes buildable land so restricted, such land sells at a premium. The developer makes all his money by taking a site of little value and then obtaining planning permission to put as many homes on it as he can. There is no incentive to include public space or shared facilities; there is no incentive to build high-quality buildings. That's all because from the moment planning permission is obtained and the site value is increased, any further cost of construction just eats into the developer's profits. It's a crude model but it's true, and it has resulted in 40 years of gimcrack housing and the creation of entire suburban areas of housing that are social deserts, dormitories dependent on intensive car use.

Although change is difficult to accept and adapt to, there's no doubt that the environmental adaptations we are going to have to make in the next 20 years, the 'culture change' of moving to a low-carbon economy – and for that matter a zero-waste and resource-frugal society – is going to hit us fast. It is very hard to deal with change when it comes quickly and repeatedly. I often feel that people aren't helped here, because change is seen as alien and often represents a degradation of people's environments. An electricity company comes along and sticks a pylon up in the middle of a well-loved view. A new housing development goes up and your street is covered in lorry mud for a year and then more cars as residents move in. Change hardly ever seems to produce a new pretty view or more trees or less noise.

A SENSE OF HISTORY

As house builders, my business and the architects and landscape architects we employ have a responsibility to provide for local needs – all of them. Which means extracting as much sense and narrative out of a place as possible in order to make a scheme feel special and rooted to where it is. If Hab ends up being involved in transforming green fields into a housing estate, the first thing we have to do is enshrine every tree and hedge and fit the houses in between. We have to use the field gates as the cues for our roads and the streams as the lines of our watercourses. Why? Because that way we can keep a sense of the history of this place and the history of its use, which all adds up to a more intelligent narrative or understanding of what it has been. The medieval word is 'palimpsest' – meaning a document on parchment that has been scraped clean of the ink of a previous use but which retains a shadow of what was there. That historical understanding provides proper context and

meaning in a place. It makes it feel special and authentic, even if that place was constructed only last week. And I believe that context and meaning (as opposed to chaos and alienation, so commonly experienced in the built environment) make fertile ground on which to provide some belonging and even self-esteem.

Not many developers take this approach, however, with the result that the idea of development remains anathema to most Brits. We are a nation of conservationists. We are now the most populous country in Europe, at 395 people per square kilometre, and we have always struggled to accommodate our population and our conservative, nature-loving instinct on the same island.

That instinct is expressed in a sentimental attachment to natural beauty, the poems of Wordsworth, the landscape of the National Trust and the 'green belts' of land that are enshrined in planning law as the restraining rings around the girth of our towns. It is that instinct which led to the growth of 'garden cities' in the early 1900s. It is that instinct which now leads me to want to conserve as much as possible of the palimpsest and context of a green field if I build houses on it.

Yet our preconceptions about what the green belt has to offer us are as wrong as our muddled thinking about the biodiversity of inner cities. The open countryside round our cities and towns is intensively farmed, using vast quantities of chemical fertilizer, pesticide and herbicide.

66 **That historical understanding provides proper context and meaning in a place. It makes it feel special and authentic** 99

GREEN BELTS

Access through this chemical monoculture is strictly controlled: although we feel we should enjoy the right to roam, in truth this is possible only in wildernesses, the National Parks and mountains where someone's livelihood is not dependent on a maximum acreage of crop being gathered in. In truth the battle for ownership and control of the green belts was won a long time ago by the agri-businesses. We can look at it out of our car window as we drive past, which is about as much as is worth doing, because the view from the car seat is no less sterile than the experience of walking through it, and in health terms frankly a lot safer.

Intimately and psychologically bound to that idea of the green belt is the idea of space. That somehow, as residents of highly dense urban environments or of mind-numbingly repetitive suburbs, we have the right to access, thanks to the car, a world of green fields, woods and blue sky in which our chests can expand and our souls can sing. Space has become a right now. We demand access to it as though it were as necessary as food or drink. Together with light, space has become the principal obsession of homeowners in the 21st century, part of the lexicon of modern builders, and for this we have to thank Le Corbusier, who asserted that light and space are as essential as food and drink.

SPACE RACE

Meanwhile, in America space has, throughout the 20th century, represented an objective to conquer, whether it was the space of the space race or the open terrestrial spaces of the vast United States. Unhampered by lack of land and the concomitant planning restrictions that brings, American developers could jump on the road bandwagon, thanks to extraordinary, large-scale infrastructure schemes put in by the likes of Robert Moses in New York in the 1920s and 30s, which saw the creation and expansion of suburbs set dozens of miles from the centre of Manhattan, made possible by car use. In Los Angeles, which in 1915 already had a sophisticated electric rail network and one car for every eight residents (the average being one car to every 43 people), the roadway was paved for massive suburbanization through the sleepy villages and orange groves of the surrounding countryside.

Space was no longer unobtainable for the city dweller. It was no longer just a psychological idea but became a reality for every homeowner. And despite the problems that space has brought us in the 20th century – total reliance on the car and a breakdown in sense of neighbourhood and community being just two – it remains one of the great talismanic romantic notions of architecture. We still equate space and light with health, happiness and physical well-being. We demand spacious rooms with spacious windows to allow healing light to variously flood, wash, inundate and scrub us clean.

The green belt, the right to roam, open space, interior space, light and generosity in a building: these are all very Western and very modern ideas. But they are privileges, not rights. They can be enjoyed only in relatively wealthy societies that need large quantities of machinery and fossil fuel to work. And drains too. Good drains make all the difference.

PRINCIPLE
35

Modern housing
should be light,
ecological,
affordable,
flexible, beautiful
and capacious.

Early computer renderings of The Triangle in Swindon (this page and overleaf) – the designs are informed by a strong sense of community, a belief in the importance of public space, respect for cyclists and pedestrians, and a commitment to sustainable lifestyles and outstanding contextual design.

HAB HOUSING

I started Hab because I felt that housing even in Britain was wrong. For decades developers have thrown up dense packs of houseburgers that are conceived, designed and sold simply as a product. The developer builds, sells and then leaves town for his next project. Sites are often miles from anywhere, requiring a lot of car use. The homes themselves are pattern-book stuff with too many circulation spaces and tiny rooms. There are fiddly details that are meant to evoke a quality 'period' feeling but which are too badly finished or designed to do that. Above all, the housing estates of the past 50 years seem so often devoid of character, any sense of place and coherence of community.

Hab focuses specifically on provincial and suburban housing projects where we feel that the standard of many current developments is particularly poor. We don't want to create ring-fenced ghettos but to focus on the social and physical relationships between our projects and the wider community in order to bring tangible improvements to both. To do that we have to work closely with the local community to establish how this can best be done and to concentrate on the space between houses as much as on the houses themselves.

Designing eco-homes is not that difficult. The building, insulating and energy technologies are there already and coming down in price as we scale up the numbers of homes we build to ever-increasing standards. However, building an eco-home that is also affordable and glamorous is trickier and requires brilliant minds and clever, elegant solutions. Building eco-homes that provide a potential new community of people with all the rich fertile ground in which to form social relations between themselves and with surrounding existing residents is the hard thing. But not impossible.

Our first trick is to work with social housing organizations: housing associations who build and finance schemes and who are covenanted into a project as its maintenance body, and who will be around in the long term to help manage and maintain the built environment and support the people living there. Our second is to grant every household, whether they rent, are in a rent-to-buy scheme or have bought their home outright, a share in the ownership of the public realm around their houses and flats. They become equal stakeholders in their environment and thus take control of its management and its future. If they want to dig up the communal kitchen garden and convert it to parking, it's a decision they can collectively take.

Third, we employ landscape architects. So what? you say; so do most developers. The difference with us is that a Hab landscape architect is granted the same control over a scheme as the architect. In their hands rests every major component of good social sustainability: the parking layout; the community orchard; drainage and the treatment of water run-off with reed beds; social spaces; hierarchy of pedestrian and car use; bicycle storage; communal recycling facilities; edible hedgerows; highways negotiations; play spaces; green roofs; car club parking and availability;

biodiversity; kitchen gardens and a local food network; crating of rainwater for washing cars and watering plants; street lighting; crime reduction. These can all be designed into a scheme or they can all be left out. They make the difference between a project of eco-homes and a sustainable community.

Our fourth trick is to be as diverse as we can in working with existing communities, in selecting tenants and in advertising to purchasers. We like to see a mix of ages in a street, from the very young to the very old. We like to provide a mix of tenure in order to encourage a wide-ranging community; for example, we target key workers in the local area, people like teachers, nurses and police staff, people who want to own. We do this in order to avoid volume turnover of the stock, which can be damaging to the community. Also, to help residents, we work with energy suppliers and with mortgage companies to devise easy, affordable ways for rental occupiers to buy and part-buy their homes in the longer term.

Our fifth trick is to sift the technology, the architecture and the public-realm design through the sieve of context.

Through researching the stories, geography, local characters, history of occupation, landmarks, local building types and other unique qualities of a place, I believe that it is possible to build up a social pattern book of that locality, full of layers of meaning, which can be used to enrich a design and make it feel entirely appropriate to where it is. It's what architects are taught to do but very rarely carry out with any real enthusiasm. It is called 'local distinctiveness' or 'narrative' and it gives brand-new places some meaning; we hope it means that residents become sooner and more attached to a place and that such a community of people becomes more socially sustainable.

And our sixth trick is a principle we believe in as an absolute necessity if our communities are going to meet future consumption requirements. Sharing. This overarching idea is an irresistible one if we are to look for ways to make life less wasteful and less resource intensive. It also sidesteps the unpalatable alternative: that we should deprive ourselves of the material comforts and benefits that we prize.

COMMUNITY

From visiting the slums of India and other communities, I know now that a community is a very loose and variable thing. It might be 10,000 people who don't know each other but who do the same job. It might be a geographical area that some New Urbanist or NGO idiotically outlines in red on a map. It might be a non-existent high rise that'll get built in 2035. It can be five houses, or more likely it can be a meaningful neighbourhood of 20 to 30 family homes where people know each other. I also know that space is not finite but elastic. You can stretch the space you own into the public realm and everybody can co-own that public realm and populate it. And then retract on to their porches and behind their front doors at night. Even the threshold can move from the front door up the stairs to the private rooms of families. We could treat and share space in the same way in our culture, couldn't we? We don't necessarily need to allocate uses to rooms or spaces in our homes. Why can't a bedroom be multi-use? Teenagers in the West already specialize in this.

I also know now that people are more important than environment in providing pleasure, solace and comfort; that well-being can be unrelated to space, convenience, facilities, leisure time, material goods, standard of living and even quality of life. But the social connectedness of small communities, the support of extended family and the network of relationships in a place are more important. These things are all forms of sharing. The glue that sticks people together – the glue that is always so strong in adversity and hardship – is produced by people together.

Chapter Seventeen

RECYCLING & REUSING

I'm writing this on a new laptop, my third in a year. The first broke irretrievably and has by now been recycled into liquid-metal Terminator parts; the second was stolen, along with my briefcase, last Tuesday while I was waiting for a train. It too is now being recycled, or rather reconditioned, for a new owner. Such are the joys of public transport.

So that my new machine does not also get nicked, I've decided to disguise it by replacing my Italian leather briefcase not with anything as posh but with a pedestrian-looking shopping bag. This, I hope, will encourage future thieves to ignore my train-spotter luggage in favour of the Italian bag of the man in the black suit to my left on platform 14.

The new shopping bag is in fact a piece of designer luggage in disguise. It's a Freitag bag, made by the brothers Freitag (ex-cycle couriers) in their factory in Zurich, out of super-durable old tarpaulins off the side of trucks, with handles cut from lengths of old seat belt. So it is almost 100 per cent recycled, or rather reconditioned into a new object, a new incarnation. Every truck tarpaulin can yield dozens of bags, so I guess my model is an example of upcycling, whereby the value of the recycled goods gets intensified, not debased.

You might prefer the word proudly chosen by the brothers Freitag: recontextualization. Golly, there's an idea. Put something in a different place and it assumes a whole other meaning. Like 1970s dark-wood Scandinavian furniture from a junk shop that can appear the acme of trendiness in a loft apartment: in most people's houses it would just look like one of your mother's cast-offs. Or vintage retro clothing, which in my day was called the 'Oxfam look'. I now see that laptops 1 and 2 were both recontextualized and that laptop 2 was socially recontextualized.

It's very difficult to recontextualize buildings, though. It's difficult to move them, for a start. They can be recycled, which usually means downcycling them and grinding them into hardcore – although the exceptions might be timber-panelled or oak-framed structures, which can be dismantled and rebuilt like a jigsaw. Old buildings can also be reconditioned and repaired and, frankly, not enough of that is done because people just can't see beyond what they are: often smelly, damp and difficult. They see a dirty old tarpaulin, not a funky bag. But if they can't be recontextualized, buildings can be given new lives in their old skins

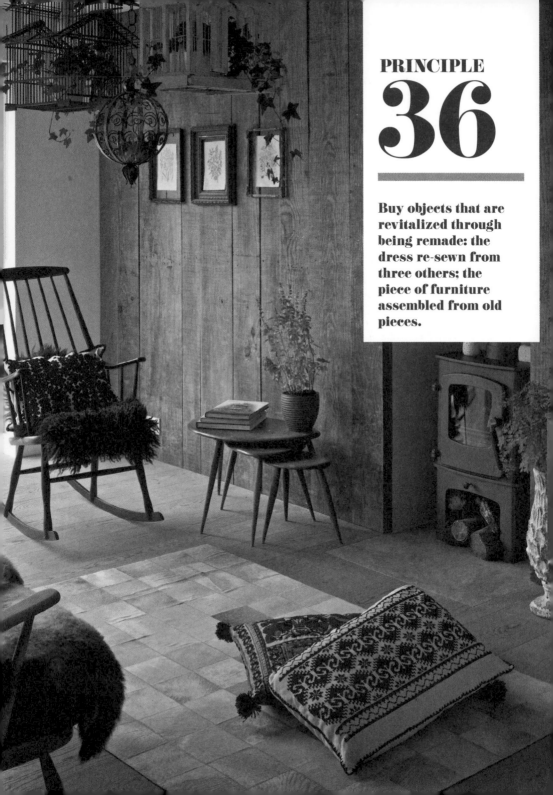

Buy objects that are revitalized through being remade: the dress re-sewn from three others; the piece of furniture assembled from old pieces.

in a process described as 'the creative reuse of buildings', a good Anglo-Saxon term that is infinitely preferable to 'recontextualization' and which recognizes the importance of activity in a building. It's all very well saving an old structure, but if there's nothing going on inside it, the place will shortly be doomed.

All this puts me in mind of the slogan on the side of my local recycling van, which extols how we should 'reduce, reuse, repair, recycle'. There's an obvious hierarchy here because the recycling of stuff, whether a plastic water bottle or a building, is energy intensive and often debases the value of the original item. In the case of a building it certainly debases the human energy, craftsmanship and commitment that goes into making a place and destroys the historic contribution that a building might make to a local sense of place.

Meanwhile, reusing and repairing old buildings, treating them gently as we do so, is an honourable activity. Just as reusing a bicycle and repairing a watchstrap are honourable. Looking after old buildings reflects well on us because it demonstrates how we value their contribution to the built environment and – much more so than recycling – reminds us how we are just guardians, not owners of our environment, whether that environment is man-made or natural.

Just as recycling buildings is a form of sharing them with previous and future generations, so recycling furniture, plastics and empty Beaujolais bottles is a form of sharing materials, goods or resources with other human beings. Here are some forms of involving yourself in the recycling loop that you may not have thought of.

66 Looking after old buildings reflects well on us because it demonstrates how we value their contribution to the built environment. 99

COMPOST

Here's an interesting fact from the Stockholm Environment Institute at the University of York: an average household that composts its kitchen and garden waste can prevent emissions of 13 kilograms of methane per year (which would result from sending the waste to landfill), equivalent to 280 kilograms of carbon dioxide (CO_2) – which is just over a quarter of a tonne – every year. That's the same amount of CO_2 that a small car produces travelling 1,000 miles.

Composting, if you haven't heard of it, is an exceptionally good way of recycling waste peelings, garden cuttings and all those packaged fruit and vegetables you bought from the supermarket and then forgot to eat. Time was when you could give waste food to your pig; in the Second World War, each street would keep a pig to feed this way. Nowadays I have a council which collects all my food waste, cooked and uncooked, including meat and bones, which is dumped in polytunnels 10 miles away to make compost. It's even possible to compost domestic waste in high-density urban environments, thanks to a New Zealand invention, the vertical composting unit (VCU), which can produce up to 25 tonnes of sweet-smelling garden fertilizer a week.

You could buy a wormery for the non-meat, non-cooked contents of your waste bin; or a fancy revolving composter; but my friend the non-dig gardening guru Charles Dowding recommends building your own composter out of cracked and disused pallets, if you have the space. I've done this and it seems to work perfectly well.

MAKE FUEL
AT HOME

This is really exciting because I'm talking not about squashing newspapers down to make bricks to burn on your hearth, but about turning old chip-fat oil into diesel. If you drive a high mileage, consider investing in a plant that will process the waste oil from deep-fat fryers into a useable fuel. The plant costs start at around £1,300 (from www.biodiesel-fuel.co.uk) and, depending where you live, there are tax breaks available. Or you could do as I do, if you're lucky enough to live near a commercial processor, and swap the filling station forecourt for an industrial estate down the road. I buy my bio-diesel ready filtered.

RING UP YOUR
FAMILY...

Offer your family all the stuff you don't want or need. Don't hang on to that heirloom bed if your niece could really do with it. Unused shirts or a dress that doesn't quite fit any more? There may be younger members of the family who'd be grateful for them. I find the best hierarchical approach is: try family first, and then friends and neighbours, before taking the rest to the charity shop and the rags to the recycling centre. Although rags are useful for polishing the car/cleaning the bicycle/wiping paintbrushes/de-grubbing the dog.

BUY SOME TOOLS AND LEARN HOW THINGS ARE MADE

OK, I'm still struggling with more than elementary sewing and I can't resolder a circuit board as my father could, but we could all of us do with learning a few basic life skills. For repairing electrical items, toys, bicycles, phones and iPods (replacement batteries are cheap and the web abounds with instructive videos on how to take these things apart) I find the most useful items are:

PRINCIPLE
37

Buy some tools and learn how to mend things. Learn to repair to polish, stitch, paint and refinish. Repair and reuse what you own and invent new uses for things.

- A set of miniature screwdrivers (an additional selection of weird-shaped heads helps)

- Pliers of all kinds and sizes

- A roll of duct tape

- Electrical tape

- Double-sided tape or stickies

- Some Velcro. Indispensible

- Socket set – including mini-sockets for tiny bolts

- Modestly sized cordless drill

- Cable ties in several sizes

- Super glue and two-part glue for mending ceramics and glass

- A needle for sewing leather, with strong thread

- Self-tapping screws for all those plastic threads that break

- A stout craft knife

- A reamer (you had better look this one up) for making holes

- Really strong reading glasses

- An afternoon

BUY PRODUCTS MADE FROM RECYCLED MATERIALS

It sounds obvious, doesn't it? Yet I still find that recycled toilet paper sits in an unloved corner of the supermarket aisle. I can buy only a limited amount of garden gravel made from smashed-up recycled toilets, because the supply of this material is still patchy. As to other domestic consumables, you may be surprised to learn that cheaper, disposable plastic goods like scourers, kitchen sponges and clothes pegs are made from virgin plastics. One British company, EcoForce, swims against this current, manufacturing these items from recycled materials. About time.

When you start to buy recycled goods and materials, an interesting thing happens: you start to get picky. For example, I'm currently looking at a new material called EcoSheet, a plywood replacement made from waste plastics of all kinds, melted down. When I say looking at it, there's a sample sitting on my desk. It's black, with a random, cellular core, and I suspect that, given the indeterminate mix of plastics in it, it could be remelted to form some new EcoSheet, but precious little else. During a week I spent working in India's plastics recycling industry, I learned that manual sorting and washing of junk plastic is essential in order to keep each waste stream free from impurities. Which leaves me somewhat depressed that this sample is of some bottom-feeding plastic, a low-performing blend of materials that can never be re-extracted for any purpose higher than as a

fencing material. It's an example of the worst kind of recycling: downcycling.

But here's an example to warm the recontextualized cockles of any recycler's heart. We consume vast quantities of ludicrously expensive water from plastic polyethylene (PET) bottles. This is not a sustainable thing to do but it does at least mean that vast quantities of PET bottles accumulate, making it relatively easy to sort them, bag them up, melt them down and spin the PET into fleece that can be used to make cheap clothes and also formed into wads that can then be sold as loft insulation. This is the noble transformation of a disposable and distasteful object into a product of indefinite life that is doing a really useful, energy-saving job every day. It's an example of the best kind of recycling: upcycling.

GET TO KNOW YOUR LOCAL BLACKSMITH & CARPENTER

In the hands of the right individual, door locks can be refettled, fencing repaired, gates rewelded, a car exhaust made whole, furniture glued and broken objects given a new steel-reinforced life. I rebuilt two woodburning stoves with the help of my local blacksmith. He also made some gates for me and converted an old children's bicycle into a lethal snow-bike for tobogganing.

BUY JUNK ART

Not bad art: junk art, made from rubbish. The work of Robbie Rowlands, Tim Noble and Sue Webster and the extraordinary trash people of H.A. Schult are all excellent examples of upcycling. Recontextualizing even.

APPROACH PREGNANT WOMEN, WITH CAUTION...

and offer them the unused pram, playmat, cradle or buggy. Many towns have a shop or two specializing in recycled babywear and equipment. If you are a man, I suggest you do not approach unaccompanied pregnant women that you do not know, at all.

Comfort in Sadness – a sliced-up bathtub transformed into a visually arresting sculpture by Melbourne-based artist Robbie Rowlands

BUY AN OLD HOUSE

This can seem almost as wasteful as buying expensive art or digging a hole, filling it with money and setting fire to it, because old houses are expensive to maintain and very old houses are very expensive to maintain. However, the care and repair of an old place is a giant exercise in recycling and mending, two of the most honourable activities it is possible to indulge in. You get greeny points for protecting culture and heritage and added greeny points for attempting low-carbon retrofitting of extra insulation, secondary glazing and ground-mounted solar panels.

RECYCLING OTHER PEOPLE'S FOOD

In his extensively researched book *Waste*, Tristram Stuart makes the simple points that, as consumers, we throw away a third of the food that we buy and that the culture of waste extends right through the food-supply market, from growers to transport companies and the large retailers. He also extols the virtue of freeganism, which includes 'dumpster diving', the art of rummaging through the bins behind supermarkets. Tristram himself lives extremely well this way and, to prove his point, turned up at a conference where we were both speaking having just jumped off the train and made his way to the venue via a local co-operative store. He arrived onstage with bags groaning with what looked like a week's shopping: bread, pastries, cream and preserves all well before their sell-by date, and vegetables and fruit that looked in peak condition. This kind of waste is shameful and we should tell our supermarkets so. In the meantime, get round to the back of the store and have a good rummage.

JOIN A RECYCLING NETWORK

This is social recycling, where you advertise your unwanted goods and possessions in your neighbourhood or region using any one of the many websites dedicated to this sensible activity. Be warned, though: you may be distracted by the free goods offered by other people and end up accumulating more than you dispose of.

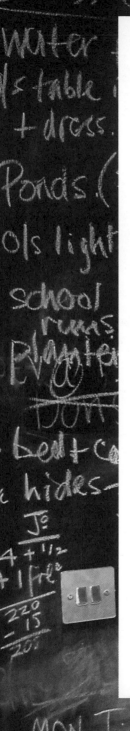

UPCYCLE INSTEAD OF RECYCLE

Look, don't allow yourself to buy bottled water just because the plastic will get recycled into loft insulation, but do remember the principle of upcycling: turn rubbish into sculpture, the useless into the useful. Tirex is a low-energy and beautiful carpet made by minimally processing pieces of car tyre. I continue to make minimalist cupboard-door handles and bookmarks from the robust, matt plastic from disused detergent bottles and gravy stock from chicken bones. Sensible.

DON'T RECYCLE

Throw nothing useful away if you can help it and wear your clothes until they are rags. I have a perfectly wealthy relative who does just this and who relishes the enriched relationship he has with his wardrobe as a result. His wife is the measure of thrift and even has separate old boxes for pieces of string recycled from packaging, marked 'string – long', 'string – short' and 'string – miscellaneous lengths'. They both grew up during the Second World War. They represent an extreme but admirable example of thrift, a value we have lost.

RECONTEXTUALIZE SOMETHING

Re-cover a dining-chair seat or make a cushion cover out of an old coat from a charity shop. Make a dress from an old pair of curtains or make an entire children's wardrobe out of drapes as Maria did in *The Sound of Music*. Make bird scarers for the vegetable garden out of old CDs.

ABOVE: A 'green' house made from recycled bottles

38

Buy less. Because, frankly, not only do we all need less but, if we're honest with ourselves, we all desire less.

REUSE SOMETHING

Bathwater can water the garden, rainwater can flush the toilet and wash the car. The shoes I bought in 1985 are now back in fashion.

REPAIR SOMETHING

Buy a macho set of needles to repair leather. Buy glue and tools to repair furniture and toys, cracked vases and shoes. Reheel shoes for that matter – or have them reheeled. Study the online guides to repairing mobile phones or the tutorial at Maplin for how to replace the battery in an iPod. Learn how to weld or rivet, how to thread a bolt and replace the washer in a tap. Sew in front of the television; sewing, knitting and television are made for each other.

DISMANTLE SOMETHING

If something doesn't work, take it apart – carefully – to understand what makes it tick. You have nothing to lose, unless there are large labels warning of danger of electric shock from internal electronic components like capacitors, which can deliver hefty jolts even after machinery has been switched off and unplugged. I'm talking about children's toys and vacuum cleaners. You can only mend something when you understand how it works.

HOARD

Don't throw useful stuff away. Keep components, plugs, bits and bobs. I dismantle old bust hair dryers, toys and broken bicycles for the nuts, bolts, screws and washers that I can glean from them before the carcass goes off to be recycled. These bits are invaluable.

PRINCIPLE

39

Zero waste is not fairytale pie in the sky. With proper municipal waste programmes, thrift and prudence, it is possible.*

*One Planet Living objective

Stonefridge – a life-sized replica of Stonehenge made out of approximately 200 recycled fridges by Santa Fe artist and filmmaker Adam Horowitz

DON'T THROW STUFF AWAY; DO GIVE STUFF AWAY

Just give it away. Don't try to sell everything. The value of a gift can be infinitely greater than the same object when sold.

AVOID AS MUCH STUFF AS POSSIBLE

We are just the guardians of plastic bags, not the owners. Avoid accumulating useless things in the first place. They may be around for a lot longer than you.

ALL RIGHT, THEN, AS A LAST RESORT: RECYCLE

Because some things really do need to be reclaimed from the waste stream. Batteries, for instance. The average household uses 21 batteries a year. The UK generates 20,000–30,000 tonnes of general-purpose waste batteries every year (excepting car batteries, which are readily recycled), but fewer than 1,000 tonnes are recycled. When disposed of incorrectly, batteries can leach heavy metals into the ground water as the casings corrode. Cadmium, for example, can be toxic to aquatic invertebrates and can bio-accumulate in fish, which damages ecosystems and makes them unfit for human consumption.

18

Chapter Eighteen

SHARING

We share our lives with others. We share the lives of loved ones more so. We share food, wine, time together, holidays, stories, a roof, a bed and library books with other people. In religious communities and hippy groups, a lot more is shared – sometimes a spouse or a dedication or sacrifice. We share our goods and clothes by passing them on to others and by recycling them. We share our homes through the dimension of time with previous and future owners. We share space on the street, in the bus and on the beach.

Sharing may seem second nature, part of the happy obligation of every family or household, but it is surprising how much in our lives we do not share and yet could, so easily. I believe that in the next 20 to 30 years we're going to have to learn how to share a great deal more. Why? First, because as the planet's population becomes larger, it stresses the Earth's resources more. I've written elsewhere in this book about how reserves of fresh water, mineral extraction biomass, coal and oil are steadily depleting. Meanwhile our ecological footprint is increasing. The WWF Living Planet Report of 2004 concluded that in 2001 our needs exceeded the biological capacity of the planet by 21 per cent. In 2008, the updated WWF report showed that the figure had risen to 25 per cent. We need to figure out how we can reverse that trend by wasting less and sharing more.

Second, sharing is something we do anyway. It is a way in which we can express ourselves as caring, social creatures. And as such, it offers the capacity to relieve the collective burden of reducing our carbon and resource footprints by spreading out ownership of those footprints. It might, for example, relieve the pressure to change our lives at an uncomfortable rate as our climate becomes more unpredictable and the pressure from governments – in the form of carbon taxes and laws limiting our behaviour – becomes less tolerable. We can endure all sorts of privations through sharing what we have and still maintain a good quality of life; we could even improve our quality of life by interacting more with those around us and enjoying the experience of sharing with them. Sharing offers us a way out of the environmental problem we face. A problem shared is a problem halved.

So it looks as though the acts of giving and receiving – sharing – could improve our sense of connection to each other and improve our communities. As well as reduce our burden on the planet. Here are some examples of sharing that I've come across that build on the precedent set by library books.

SHARED HOUSING

Dotted around the Western hemisphere are little groups of like-minded souls who aim to share as much as consensually can be agreed in their community. In some cases, ownership of their homes is shared between them or with a housing association or other social landlord. This is the kind of scheme that my business, Hab, is encouraging; our social-housing partners, GreenSquare Group, offer part-ownership (where the resident jointly owns a home with the landlord and jointly splits profits with them when they sell) and rent-to-buy schemes (where the resident pays some monthly rent on top of a deposit of, say, 25 per cent of the full value of the home with a view to buying more of the home, up to 100 per cent of its value, as time passes and finances ease).

But the really interesting end of shared housing is not about ownership but activity, where much more is shared. Food is often grown communally and even cooked and eaten together, with families or households taking it in turn to prepare a meal and clear up afterwards. Springhill Cohousing in Stroud, Gloucestershire, is one such community, organized around the co-housing principles of collective decision making, pedestrianized streets, a communal house for shared evening meals and private dwellings for each household. A number of committees, covering, for example, the kitchen, the garden, parking and disputes, are mandated to make decisions and govern the scheme. Residents confess that the shared arrangements give them more leisure time and a more economical way of life as a result of domestic tasks not being duplicated. I have to admit being heavily influenced by Springhill in planning the new housing developments that Hab is building across the west of England.

LAUGH

The Nobel-prize-winning president of the Institute of Cell Physiology, Dr Otto Warburg, has said: 'Deep breathing techniques which increase oxygen to the cell are the most important factors in living a disease free and energetic life.' Dr Michael Miller, director of the Center for Preventive Cardiology at the University of Maryland Medical Centre, has said: 'The old saying that "laughter is the best medicine" definitely appears to be true when it comes to protecting your heart.'

Laughter can improve serotonin levels, boost the immune system and cheer other people up. You can join a laughter club or log on to www.sharinglaughter.com. Or go out with a mate for a pint. Or chat over a cup of tea with a neighbour. Or watch re-runs of *Trading Places* with Dan Ayckroyd and Eddie Murphy.

Laugh and the world laughs with you. Cry and you cry alone. Laugh alone and you probably need to see someone.

WORK SHARE

This is not a new way of behaving. It dates back to the time when slaves worked a 24-hour shift sharing the role of looking after one master. Nowadays, two working mums can voluntarily share the responsibilities of one full-time job, and receive their salary and benefits on a pro-rata basis. Job sharing creates regular part-time work that often fits the patterns of people's lives better than full-time work and can mitigate a total loss of employment in a layoff.

PRINCIPLE
40

Don't own stuff. Lease a house; borrow tools – but do return them; beg a cup of sugar now and then; hire a drill when you need it. Don't buy, don't be proud and don't try to be too independent.

A KITCHEN GARDEN – THE NEW ALLOTMENT

There are some who prefer not to watch the game on TV but to get outside, beat their breast and grow some vegetables, one of the last honourable activities known to man. Traditionally this was done by renting a small patch of land or digging up a piece of one's own garden. Increasingly, however, this individual approach is being replaced by more communal gardening methods.

Guerrilla gardening – the practice of cultivating someone else's barren land without their permission (usually redundant building sites) – hasn't yet taken off across the whole planet in the same way that it has on the streets of New York, but the blistering increase in allotment applications during the recent recession is testament to how the British like to redistribute the wealth of our land. As is the swelling interest in land share, where growers are put in touch with landowners with fallow land; 45,000 are subscribed at the time of writing.

But for some, this is not enough. Research from the University of Leeds, published in *Trends in Ecology and Evolution*, calls for us to chop down the leylandii hedge and smudge the red boundary line. We're told that if we act together we can create wildlife corridors through suburbia. If we collaborate and coordinate with our neighbours we can form interlinking habitats, increase biodiversity and encourage more birds, mammals and insects. We need, it seems, to start gardening ecologically and collectively.

I don't know if we're ready to break down the larch-lap and merge our gardens, but I intend to find out. In Swindon, my company, Hab, is offering residents both small private gardens and larger shared spaces in collective ownership. We're letting people own the fruit trees on the corner of the street and the polytunnel in the allotment – or kitchen garden, as we fondly refer to it. Plans for future projects include private gardens shared between a dozen or so households. Although we would find it difficult to knock a row of houses into one and share our private dwellings, I think we'd find it refreshing and rewarding – and so, it seems, would the wildlife, if we gardened with biodiversity in mind and shared our land. Even a little. I'll be the first to visit the suburban street where the residents have demolished half their fencing and co-garden a shared strip of biodiverse, organically managed land running behind their houses. I might even buy them a shed.

A SHED

A FOOD NETWORK

The shed is the last refuge of the household man, *Homo domesticus*. Consequently, no self-respecting sustainability campaigner would ever dare suggest that a man shares his shed with someone else. I wouldn't. But I would suggest building a separate communal shed on a street. Here's why. According to Bioregional, the average power tool gets used for four minutes – in its entire life. We are obviously a society of aspirant DIY-ers, but we are also obviously too lazy to stop watching the match and get our butts off the couch to go and do any. Is there a possibility this might change? I don't think so. Should we instead be clubbing together and buying for each street a drill, a shed, a sanding machine and a couple of lawnmowers? Of course we should. The stuff would get used, countless hours would be frittered away in the shed talking about torque settings and how to make compost with grass clippings and cardboard, and we'd save money.

This is really an extension of the allotment, kitchen garden or co-gardening principle. You grow your own. You barter the glut of your produce – some courgettes for some blackcurrants or some of a neighbouring farmer's lamb even. Others do the same; one or two even sell their honey or produce. A few might even join local professional growers at a local farmers' market every week. One of those farmers gets a local box scheme going, enriched with produce from other cultivators. Then a shop springs up at a local farm as an almost-serious rival to the local supermarket. Bingo! You've got the makings of a local food network.

I have a fanciful notion, but not an impracticable one, that one day the average-sized town in Europe, Australia or America will be largely self-sustaining in food terms: growing much of what it needs within a radius of, say, 30 miles, the food fertilized by the waste from that town and grown in facilities sometimes warmed by the waste heat from a waste-to-energy or biomass combined heat and power station. Produce will be shipped in to a central depot on a daily basis and then distributed to a network of 20 or 30 shops, each selling local and regional foods. This is a miniature version of what the supermarkets already practise, only it has the advantage of being integrable into a local economy, the local supply chain, the local waste stream and local culture. It is a reproduction of how towns and cities organized themselves 300 years ago. It is also going to be necessary if we are to reduce our carbon footprint. Food growing and transportation are responsible for about 20 per cent of our carbon emissions.

A FRACTIONAL LIFE

If you really can't kick the champagne and give up the Ferrari and private jet, at least consider sharing them. Fractionallife.com offers a glimpse of what it must be like to be a fabulously wealthy international traveller with a conscience. This is ethical high life with more than a whiff of hypocrisy about it. Ideal for the wives of rock musicians.

JUST GIVE UP MONEY

Food is one thing that you can barter. But there are plenty of things to swap, or at the very least trade, for goods or services in the local economy. And if you don't need anything right now, don't worry: you can collect credit or tokens and 'cash' them in sometime in the future. Babysitting, car maintenance, food, gardening help, legal advice, website design and countless other really useful activities can thus be exchanged without the need for money, tax or regulation. This makes barter very attractive to those who are unemployed on means-tested benefits and to those whose skills are more manual and less professional, because barter schemes are based primarily on time spent doing something rather than a chargeable hourly rate. Thus an accountant will perhaps barter three hours of gardening for three hours of bookkeeping. Think of barter as a halfway house between the informally valued culture of giving, as practised by the Polynesians, and the exchange of hard cash for a hard-priced commodity that we are so used to in the West. Barter is soft, friendly and, above all, local.

The more sophisticated schemes are called LETS (Local Exchange Trading Schemes), which are regulated and which usually operate over the Internet. You should look up your nearest. Some even produce their own local currency such as the Totnes pound, which cannot be banked or accrue interest. But just as the Internet is a useful tool for these schemes, so it has also become the setting for a virtual LETS scheme, timebanking (www.timebank.co.uk), which operates on as wide a scale as you want it to and which is subscribed to by tens of thousands of volunteers, the majority of whom are under 25.

FURNITURE AND GOODS

Time was when human beings never had enough of anything. Then there was a time when there was just enough and we made good by mending and repairing what we had. This was followed, quite quickly, by a time of plenty when we saw possessions as consumables and forgot how to mend things, throwing away stuff when it stopped working or when we became a size too big for it. Hot on its heels came the time of ludicrous consumerism when we bought things only on the understanding that they were disposable, so we could buy some more stuff soon. Now it appears, pray God, that we have the possibility of entering a period of reflection, in which we can thoughtfully dispose of what we don't need in the knowledge that other people might need it. Websites like www.freecycle.org allow us to get rid of unwanted possessions; old school uniforms go to second-hand shops, toys get given to the library. We can share what we have rather than just dump it.

PRINCIPLE 41

Consider taking joint ownership with your neighbours of the street and shared spaces outdoors. Share control of where you live; share responsibility for how your street is used and share resources: an allotment, tools, a workshop or play equipment.

PRINCIPLE 42

Streets, as part of the public realm, should be the domain of people and cyclists, not just cars.

OWNING YOUR OWN STREET

Our obsession with bureaucratic neatness has eroded ambiguous spaces from our public realm. Builders like straight lines, lawyers like clear boundaries. Developers like empty sites and simple rectilinear plans. Local authorities and the police force are united in their dislike of spaces that encourage people to loiter and lurk. The market doesn't like patches of land that can't be easily parcelled up and sold. Housing associations deliberately seek to minimize shared spaces in a quest to avoid neighbourly dispute.

But in banishing awkwardness and mess we lose the very areas where relationships are forged. Making places is about more than increasing the range of goods and services to hand. If a neighbourhood is to have its own centre of gravity, it needs an understanding of 'community' that is greater than the sum of the individual households. It needs public space and shared space: places that allow for the possibility of sharing, working together, socializing. Spaces that invite you to amble, linger, chat.

Kitchen gardens, shared vegetable plots, community buildings and car pools offer endless potential for disagreement and abuse, but they are also fundamental in transforming discrete family units into a functioning community. As with families, the most successful communities are those that can accommodate and survive a healthy dose of argument and chaos.

Social sustainability cannot be made or grown. You have to leave communities to do that. But you can leave a fertile site ready for them. Our landscape architects, Studio Engleback, have provided our projects at Hab with all the rich loam we could hope for: edible hedgerows; sensible SUDS schemes that filter water through reeds and store it for hand-pumping to vegetable gardens and for washing cars; car clubs; fruit trees; a pioneering concept that we've jointly developed of parking 'footprint'; usable social space; LED street lighting; interest, joy and delight.

And with our partners, Greensquare Group, we are pioneering the use of community trusts in which every household, whether renting or owning their property, holds one share in the ownership of the public realm. This means the spaces between buildings, the orchard and kitchen garden, social and play spaces and even car parking. In extreme examples, residents might even own the street and the street lighting, although the maintenance and care for these are often onerous and best left to local government. Importantly, ownership of land in a community land trust might extend beyond the planning boundary and the land originally designated and bought for development.

The maintenance of public realm can often be ignored. The model we are developing involves residents both as owners and as part-time stewards of what they have. A social-housing landlord will bear the brunt of the maintenance responsibility of a scheme, together with the local council, but in our experience together they find their burden eased by the enthusiasm of residents for what they have and by the

> **66 In banishing awkwardness and mess we lose the very areas where relationships are forged. 99**

fact that shared ownership of public realm means it gets looked after better in the first place. Indeed, by employing local unemployed kids as part-clients/part-installers on public-realm projects like play equipment, it's possible to neutralize potential vandalism. I've seen very persuasive projects to this effect in regeneration schemes of gardens and parks in Castleford, Yorkshire, where local schoolchildren of mixed ages were given the task of planting several thousand flowering bulbs as well as designing their own signage and playspaces. It worked. You don't trash what you own. You certainly don't trash what you've invested in.

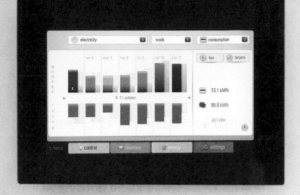

INFORMATION

If you consider yourself progressive, you may have a smart meter in your home that measures your energy consumption and tells you when you're exceeding your average. Some smart meters are impenetrably difficult to understand; others glow different colours and are as tactile and as desirable as an iPod. IBM trumpets its own evolution of this technology, which tells you how much water you're using in your home as well.

All well and good, but supposing your smart meter could tell you when the next bus is due at the bus stop round the corner? Supposing it could compare the energy performance of your home with the average for the street? Supposing that, at three in the morning, when your child has a temperature and you have no Calpol, it could alert every home in the neighbourhood and quietly ask if anybody is still up and could help?

Our home technology is still bitty. Our fridge doesn't talk to our stereo; nor should it. But our machines could do so much more for us and those living in our neighbourhood, particularly when hooked up to local services, hospitals, schools and councils. Imagine a screen on your kitchen wall and an app on your mobile phone that could between them hook up to all of that information on a local intranet, sort out your babysitting or a few hours of bartered time, check on a delivery of local food or book a local tennis court or car-club vehicle. A sort of home iPhone, plugged into your community. That's the technology that we're investing in at Hab.

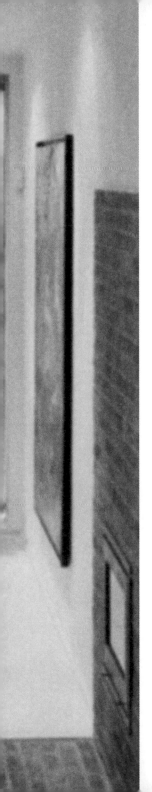

> **66 Car clubs alleviate the need for that second or third car 99**

A CAR CLUB

The precepts of a car club are simple. Most cars are not used for the vast majority of time. Many of us don't need a car every day. Many households have two or even three cars for convenience. Car clubs – which are often run as profit-making businesses – exist all over the world and are springing up in towns and cities by the dozen every month. The principles are brilliant. Thorough use of a group of shared vehicles, locally parked, rented by the hour, means fewer cars parked on the streets, fewer cars wastefully produced and less cost of ownership. Given that a car depreciates with time, and even if not driven requires servicing and maintenance, residents in a neighbourhood can be relieved of this financial drain. Car clubs alleviate the need for that second or third car and cost of membership of a club can be between a third and a half of owning your own car, without the burden of capital investment. It's a no-brainer, really.

Even simpler than a car club is the expedient and obvious way everyday journeys can be shared. Community intranets are ideal for this because they can introduce residents who might never share their car with someone to a friendly, recognizable neighbour, as opposed to a stranger found via a third-party scheme. But third-party schemes, like liftshare.com, do exist and are successful. They encourage a range of security measures such as registration of journeys on a website and the virtual sharing (online social behaviour) of favourite routes. You can also look for a buddy for your bike, walking or taxi journey. This is the web as global/local community. Anyone fancy a hike in the Hindu Kush on Thursday?

PRINCIPLE
43

**Sharing is a
fundamentally
civilized form of
behaviour that
is at the root of
sustainable living.**

THE MANUAL OF DWELLING

Aside from the 43 Principles of Home there are one or two other lists that I admire. So here, for your delectation, is Le Corbusier's Manual of Dwelling along with my own updated manual.

In the 1920s Le Corbusier gave some advice to new homeowners in *Vers une Architecture* (*Towards a New Architecture*, 1923), called the Manual of Dwelling.

66 **The existing plan of the dwelling-house takes no account of man and is conceived as a furniture store... The temperance societies and the anti-Malthusians should address an urgent appeal to architects; they should have the Manual of Dwelling printed and distributed to mothers of families and should demand the resignation of all the professors in the architectural schools.** 99

- **Demand a bathroom** looking South, one of the largest rooms in the house or the flat, the old drawing room for instance. One wall to be entirely glazed, opening if possible on to a balcony for sun baths; the most up-to-date fittings with a shower bath and gymnastics appliances.

- **An adjoining room** to be a dressing-room in which you can dress and undress. Never undress in your bedroom. It is not a clean thing to do and makes the room horribly untidy. In this room demand fitments for your linen and clothing not more than 5 feet in height, with drawers, hangers etc.

- **Demand one** really large living room instead of a number of small ones.

- **Demand bare walls** in your bedroom, your living room and your dining room. Built-in fittings to take the place of much of the furniture, which is expensive to buy, takes up too much room and needs looking after.

- **If you can**, put the kitchen at the top of the house to avoid smells.

- **Demand** concealed or diffused lighting.

- **Demand** a vacuum cleaner.

- **Buy only practical** furniture and never buy decorative 'pieces'. If you want to see bad taste, go into the houses of the rich. Put only a few pictures on your walls and none but good ones.

- **Keep your odds** and ends in drawers and cabinets.

- **The gramophone** or the pianola or wireless will give you exact interpretations of first-rate music, and you will avoid catching cold in the concert hall, and the frenzy of the virtuoso.

- **Demand** ventilating panes to the windows in every room.

- **Teach** your children that a house is only habitable when it is full of light and air, and when the floors and walls are clear. To keep your floors in order eliminate heavy furniture and thick carpets.

- **Demand** a separate garage to your dwelling.

- **Demand** that the maid's room should not be an attic. Do not park your servants under the roof.

- **Take a flat** which is one size smaller than what your parents accustomed you to. Bear in mind economy in your actions, your household management and in your thoughts.

THINGS TO PUT INTO YOUR HOUSE OR AN UPDATED MANUAL OF DWELLING

I think it's about time Le Corbusier's manual is updated and so below you'll find my own, written with 30 years' experience of dealing with, designing, writing about and filming homes.

In many ways this list of principles is a summary of everything this book covers: the big ideas that make homes work properly.

Why, 90 years after Le Corbusier included his list in *Vers une Architecture*, do we still need to be reminded of basic principles? Well, times change and so does the way that people live. Corb talked of sun baths and dining rooms, whereas today life is less formal and there is greater emphasis on energy use and the environment.

And we continue to make mistakes. Developers continue to build energy-hungry crap houses that are poorly laid out, badly lit and over-fussy. And we continue to buy furniture made from timbers of dubious source and clothes sewn by children in the Third World. As I write I have next to me an article in the *Independent* newspaper of this morning, 27 April 2010, in which a court victory is announced for the 1,650 victims of a toxic reaction to dimethyl fumarate, a chemical still used to treat leather in the Far East but which has been banned in the EU. A total of 4,000 customers have claimed that leather furniture they bought from highly respected high street shops in the UK produced serious health problems such as breathing difficulties, and skin and eye reactions. Some even believed they had skin cancer or were dying.

This is the price of fashion and the price we pay for an exploding global population that is demanding consumer goods and a standard of living never seen on such a widespread scale. The result is an unparalleled stress on the resources we have, leading to the invention of substitute processes and products that require synthetic chemical and fossil fuel inputs. In pursuit of what we think is desirable or right we so often make a foolish mistake or even poison ourselves. Anyway, on a much more cheerful note, the following offer something of an antidote.

- **Organize your home** life around who you are and what you do. If you have a family, enshrine what is good about that family in the layout of your building.

- **Choose the architecture**, the garden, the decoration and the furnishings around who you are, what you dream of and what has made you. The most interesting and enriching homes are those that are full of autobiography, not those that resemble furniture showrooms.

- **Organize life** around a light, open area to cook, eat, socialize and rest. Make this the Living Space, the largest room in your house. Place the television here or near by. The terms 'kitchen', 'living room' and 'dining room' are obsolete. This room should be the centre of the home, but also demand a small quiet room for study, peace, homework and reflection.

- **Do not** slavishly follow the layout of an old home. 19th-century buildings were often laid out for the convenience of the plumber. Swapping the roles of rooms can invigorate the building and improve your experience of it.

- **Do respect** the character of old buildings and cherish their idiosyncrasies and imperfections. The character of a place consists of a thousand tiny details which can carelessly be 'improved' into mediocrity.

- **Demand storage**: convenient storage for bikes, bins, buggies, toys and tools outside. Indoors, make storage above a lowered bathroom ceiling or in full-height cupboards that reach to the ceiling. Make a bank of storage, preferably on a north wall to provide an additional insulating effect. Storage can be found in the most unlikely of places. Narrow shelves on a landing will accommodate vast quantities of books, phone chargers and the bric-a-brac of life.

- **Avoid over-simplifying** your home. Human beings respond to richness, warmth, texture and complexity. But do make empty spaces on walls and on surfaces. Clutter and complexity are only tolerable when complemented by some emptiness.

- **Demand** that your home be flexible and adaptable enough to see you through your years or that there be ample chance for you to live in another suitable home near by, if you want. Communities of mixed ages are richer for it.

- **Demand** that your home consume the minimum of energy and yet keep you warm and comfortable. Demand a healthy environment with fresh, clean air. Demand that your building does not just save energy but produces it. Demand that your home has a minimal environmental footprint and uses our precious resources wisely and miserly.

- **Demand** vents that can be opened at a low level in the building and in the roof space to allow fresh, cool air to circulate and rise during hot weather.

- **Demand** to know where things come from, what is in them, who has made them and under what conditions. Do not be led by price only but look for value and craftsmanship. Buy only things and materials that respect the human energy that has gone into them and where the maker is rewarded fairly.

- **Demand** light but do not demand that the building be 'flooded' or 'drenched' in it. Light is the means whereby we make sense of our environment but works only by creating shadow. Shadow is essential and is the counterpoint to light.

- **Demand** concealed artificial lighting that provides soft background illumination. This is ideal when looking at screens. Demand task lighting directed at work surfaces for activities, but insist that light sources are concealed: avoid glare at all costs.

- **Avoid being seduced** by the trinkets and gadgets of domestic life. A glass and steel balustrade may seem exciting but a good, plasterboarded simple low wall will be much cheaper and more of a piece with the building as a whole. The real pleasure of a properly designed house lies in the arrangement of the components not decoration.

- **Make everything** you touch of the very highest quality. Door handles, locks, switches, chairs and controls should be an ergonomic pleasure to use and robust enough for that pleasure to continue.

- **Employ an interior designer** only if you have several homes and are too rich and bored to furnish them yourself. Interior design is a discipline suited to the impersonal commercial environment. What makes a home interesting are the tastes and foibles of the people who live there.

- **Spend your money** on the bones of your building: on insulation, structure, joinery, windows and airtightness. Kitchens and bathrooms may seem glamorous purchases but fall victim to fashion. All machines, regardless of price, stop working. But the building can endure and is worth investing in.

- **Accept a bedroom** that is modest in size with a lower ceiling if it affords you a larger Living Space with a higher ceiling. A bedroom need be nothing more than an embracing, comforting cell, provided there is room to dress and storage for clothes.

- **Employ the principle** of compression and release. A narrow, low and dark corridor can produce drama when it opens into a large, high, light room. Small

service rooms with plenty of storage can relieve living spaces of the mechanical clutter of day-to-day life.

- **Work with the best** people you can to produce your home. Use an architect who shares the same view of the world that you do. Employ people who understand building to help you construct your home and don't try to do everything yourself. Building a house is not a DIY project.

- **Demand** a building that is easy to walk around. Good, fluid layout and circulation are essential for well-being in a home and will enrich your enjoyment of using the space. This is a much misunderstood point. Large rooms and volumes are not the same thing as good circulation, which can be worked out on a plan.

- **Lay out** your circulation space, if you can, generously. Allow corridors to be wide enough to pass someone easily. Similarly, make your garden path wide enough for two people to stand and hold hands. Romance has to flourish somewhere.

- **Allow things to patinate**. Do not jettison the things you own because they become tired. Learn to mend, to polish, stitch, paint and refinish. Repair and reuse what you own and invent new uses for things. Accept the character that time confers and that the moment something is newly made, it starts to become old.

- **Respect the territory** of the cook. Allow the cook in the household freedom to move unimpeded from cooker to larder to fridge to work surface to sink. A good working kitchen is small and need be nothing more than a galley. Anything more is ostentation. Design the kitchen to allow the cook the opportunity to converse while cooking.

• **Devote a room** to laundry. This is a significant domestic activity. If you have no children and some space, put this room on the bedroom floor to avoid hauling laundry around the home; laundry is generated in bathrooms and bedrooms and linen can be stored on the same floor. If you have children you may prefer to put the laundry room near the kitchen and social space to allow you to juggle washing with cooking and childcare.

• **Put machines at the right height**. Human beings see the world from 5 feet 6 inches off the ground, so place machine displays at this height. Place a washing machine or oven so that the door is at elbow height and a dishwasher so that the door, when opened, is at hip height. This way you will not need to bend. Organize fitted storage on all sides of these machines to eliminate moving around when loading and unloading them. Make your world ergonomic.

• **Demand a downstairs room** as a washroom or utility room for boots, coats and the stuff of the world outside. Make this the laundry room if necessary.

• **Demand a larder** or cold room for storing foodstuffs. Make this a super-insulated space, ventilated to the outside but airtight to the indoors. Refrigerators are wasteful and bloated machines that could well occupy a fraction of the space devoted to them.

• **Make the context** of where you live part of the narrative of your home. Research local history, start a local food network, memorize your landmarks and visit the places of interest and history on your doorstep. Study the flora, fauna and geology of your place, even if it is intensely urban. Invent a story for your place.

• **Demand high-quality design** in your home and high-quality work. You deserve it and so does the building. Place faith in the design process and engage with it. Understand that drawing is an essential tool of design, not for presenting finished ideas but for exploring them and improving them. A drawing is just a mark on some paper, and an idea.

• **Demand interest** and originality in your public realm. Look for clues to its identity and celebrate the local uniqueness of where you live.

• **Consider taking joint ownership** with your neighbours of the street and shared spaces outdoors. Share control of where you live; share responsibility for how your street is used and share resources: an allotment, tools, a workshop or play equipment.

• **Follow the Principles** of Good Design according to Kev: that any man-made thing should be well made and durable, it should be ergonomic and fit for purpose, it should have brought no harm to anybody or anything and it should evoke delight and lasting pleasure in use.

INDEX